After all this time

Reflections on Jesus

Other Books by Anne Benjamin

Not Forgotten. Australian Catholic Educators 1820-2020
(edited with Seamus O'Grady, Coventry Press 2020)

Leadership in a Synodal Church
(co-authored with Charles Burford, Garratt Publishing 2021)

Saffron and Silk: An Australian in India
(David Lovell Publishing 2016)

Gemstones, an anthology of collaborative short-form poetry
(Skylark Publishing 2016)

Catholic Schools: Hope in Uncertain Times
(edited with Dan Riley, Garratt Publishing 2008)

It takes three things to attain a sense of significance:
God
a soul
and a moment
These three things are always here.
Just to be is a blessing.
Just to live is holy.

Abraham Joshua Heschel

'*Without any doubt, the mystery*
of our religion is very deep indeed.'

1 Timothy 3:16

Jesus of Nazareth was '*a strange and complex Jew*'.

John Meier, *A Marginal Jew*, Volume II, p. 970.

After all this time

Reflections on Jesus

Anne Benjamin

COVENTRY
PRESS

Published in Australia by
Coventry Press
33 Scoresby Road
Bayswater VIC 3153

ISBN 9781922589170

Copyright © Anne Benjamin 2022

All rights reserved. Other than for the purposes and subject to the conditions prescribed under the *Copyright Act*, no part of this publication may be reproduced, stored in a retrieval system, or transmitted in any form or by any means, electronic, mechanical, photocopying, recording or otherwise, without the prior permission of the publisher.

Scripture taken from the Holy Bible NEW INTERNATIONAL VERSION®, NIV®, Copyright © 1973, 1978, 1984, 2011 by Biblica, Inc.® Used with permission. All rights reserved worldwide.

And from the *New Jerusalem Bible* copyright © 1985 by Darton Longman & Todd Ltd and Doubleday, a division of Random House, Inc. Reprinted with Permission.

And from the *Saint Joseph New Catholic Bible*® Copyright © 2019 by Catholic Book Publishing Corp. Used with permission. All rights reserved.

Catalogue-in-Publication entry is available from the National Library of Australia http://catalogue.nla.gov.au

Cover design by Ian James – www.jgd.com.au
Text design by Coventry Press
Set in EBGaramond

Printed in Australia

Contents

Acknowledgments 11
Introduction 13

1 Prelude 25
   1.1 A certain place in time 25
   1.2 A young woman in Nazareth 28
   1.3 Ein Kerem 33
   1.4 Bethlehem 36

2 Early life, pre-ministry 43
   2.1 Yeshua of Nazareth 43
   2.2 Jesus and his family 46
   2.3 About God 49
   2.4 Bringing up the lad 57
   2.5 Crafting a yoke 61

3 Going public 68
   3.1 Jesus leaves home 68
   3.2 Immersion in his mission 76
   3.3 Desert and isolation 79
   3.4 Beginning his ministry 85
   3.5 Who is this man? 90

4 Yeshua: Teacher 95
   4.1 Where he worked 95
   4.2 His teaching: a kingdom of God 100
   4.3 So, what is this kingdom? 103
   4.4 Within and among us 109
   4.5 A kingdom for everyone 120
   4.6 Waiting for the kingdom 123

5	Followers, companions, disciples		130
	5.1	By your friends...	130
	5.2	Being a disciple	134
	5.3	Who took up his challenge?	138
	5.4	Joining his team	147
	5.5	The Twelve	150
6	Signs of Wonder		164
	6.1	Signs on the sea	164
	6.2	Signs of abundance	167
	6.3	Exorcism	174
	6.4	Touch	179
	6.5	His mother's only son	185
	6.6	Time to think differently	189
7	Breath of Wisdom		191
	7.1	Sophia, the Wisdom of God	191
	7.2	Finding Wisdom	196
	7.3	Wisdom from the kitchen	204
	7.4	Unexpected Wisdom	207
	7.5	Lessons for leaders	217
8	Opposition Grows		221
	8.1	Facing Jerusalem	223
	8.2	Teaching and testing	229
	8.3	Last appeal to Israel	234
	8.4	Finding strength and comfort	238
	8.5	The Law and the Sabbath	239
	8.6	A dutiful Jew with laws of love	247
	8.7	By whose authority?	252
	8.8	Betrayal	260
9	Last days		264
	9.1	Raising Lazarus	264
	9.2	Plans for his death	272
	9.3	Dinner at home with friends	273

10	Passion and death	277
	10.1 Final meal with friends	277
	10.2 Abandonment	288
	10.3 Trial	293
	10.4 Death and burial	304
11	Resurrection	310
	11.1 Mariam, first witness	310
	11.2 Walking away	313
	11.3 Back home in Galilee	318
	11.4 Peter	322
Selective Reading Guide		325

Glossary

BCE: 'Before the Common Era'. Previously called BC (Before Christ) and generally refers to the period of history before the birth of Jesus of Nazareth.

CE: 'Common Era'. Previously called AD (Anno Domini) and generally refers to the period of history following the birth of Jesus of Nazareth.

Sirach/Ecclesiasticus: Used to name the biblical book sometimes known by its author Ben Sira. It was not included in the Hebrew Scriptures, although Jews who followed Jesus used it.

NCB: New Catholic Bible

NIV: New International Version

NJB: New Jerusalem Bible

NRSVCE: New Revised Standard Version Catholic Edition

Acknowledgments

It is impossible to acknowledge comprehensively all those who have contributed to this book because their influence began in my childhood and continued through my schooling and all the years of study since. Above all, I am indebted to the inspiration of people of faith and scholars who break open the Word to me in ways that they could not imagine. I am also nourished by being part of a fellowship of poets in a companionable search for words about meaning that matters.

I was introduced to tanka poetry and to a nurturing community of tanka poets by my sister Carmel Summers, a gifted poet across different genres. Carmel is always most generous in encouraging my work – even when it is outside her usual field of interest. I continue to learn from her.

More specifically, I am grateful for the generous advice and reactions of those who gave their time and attention to reviewing the draft. Their expertise encompasses many domains and their suggestions, challenges and encouragement have been most helpful. I acknowledge:

Dr Michele Connolly, rsj
Carolyn Eldridge-Alfonzetti
Jan Foster
Rev. Robert Irwin msc
Rev. Ross Naylor
Philip Pogson
Carmel Summers
Greg Wilson

In the end, however, I take full responsibility for the final manuscript. Responsibility for errors and limitations rests entirely with me.

The book would not have been published without Hugh McGinlay, publisher at Coventry Press, who brought his considerable scholarship to bear in reading it and who was willing to trust in its merit. I thank him and the team at Coventry for the final production.

A travel grant from Australian Catholic University, made possible by former Executive Deans of the Faculty of Education and Arts, Professors Tania Aspland and Elizabeth Labone, facilitated a period of study in Israel and the Palestinian Territories. This visit followed a previous 'Light of Torah' study tour, led by Teresa Pirola and Fr Vince Casey, which provided amazing experiences and opportunities.

My friends have encouraged this project although I suspect some wondered at the wisdom of it. And as always, I have been cheered on by my husband Susai and our three children, Mariam, Shanthi and Mathew. Even if they sometimes wonder what Mum does at her desk all day, they are honest critics, my biggest supporters and most generous in celebrating my efforts.

Anne Benjamin
January 2022

Introduction

Think of someone you have loved very much. Someone who has changed you and your view of yourself and of the world. Someone who has entered your life never to leave. Such a person can lead us to see places and objects differently: a park, a particular tree, a restaurant, a cup. In their absence, such places and things can become poignant touchstones for tracing the loved one. We want to revisit the time and place. This is where... It was here on this day that...

That is why, for sixteen days in 2012, I travelled as a pilgrim through Israel and Palestine on a journey to discover more about the land in which Jesus lived. I travelled with twenty fellow Australians and enjoyed their company and good humour and the privilege of being guided by someone steeped in the land, its history and Judeo-Christian scriptures. For me, it was a personal quest to find my own understanding of Jesus Christ around whose teaching my whole life has been lived. At times, the journey was tiring but it was, for me, also too short and rich in information with never enough time to get my head around what this man Jesus means in a modern world so far removed from his time: what Jesus means in my life in Sydney, busy with family, plans and commitments.

In 2018, I returned to Israel and Palestine for a longer period to spend time in research, reflection and reading in the land where Jesus Christ lived and died.

These pages attempt to continue the pilgrimage now that I am back home in Western Sydney, to continue standing in the gift of those journeys, to make personal sense of the mystery and person of Jesus Christ. This might seem odd coming from someone who has lived and worked within the Church all her life. Who was this Jesus whose name has continued down through 2000 years in a way few others have? What was it about him that made him so different from other prophets and teachers? Why has his name and influence continued? Who is the Jesus the early followers remembered? These questions are deeply personal ones for me: they go to the core of who I am, how I construct meaning in my life.

Too often, the way we speak about Jesus has become somewhat trivial, mundane and domestic. Yet, this was a man who provoked opposition to the point of being sentenced to death. He could not have been a safe and cosy teacher. Too often our words about Jesus are trite and lifeless. Walter Brueggemann, referring to preaching, hits it on the head when he writes that the Gospel often becomes 'a truth greatly reduced, flattened, trivialised, rendered inane...'[1]

Purpose and limitations

This book does not pretend to be a comprehensive travel log or chronology of my visits. The pages that follow contain my reflections on selected moments in the story of Jesus as contained in the Gospels; there are many others not included. My hope is that these pages might speak to others as I attempt to hear my soul and God converse in these few moments. I am doing this to understand a little more about a man called Yeshua who grew to maturity in the first century of the Common Era (1CE) in a small Middle Eastern village,

---

[1] Walter Brueggemann, *Finally comes the poet*, Fortress Press, Minneapolis, 1989, pp. 1-11.

far removed from the mainstream of political and city life, within a peasant community, in a country ruled by foreign Roman rulers.

The things we know about Jesus of Nazareth are fragments only: actual words he might have used and typical actions. Scholars' explorations of this fill many volumes. We do know what his early followers recalled and understood about his teaching and actions, and so we can, with assurance, speak about 'the kind of thing' that Jesus would have said and 'the kind of thing' that Jesus would have done. These are the truths of Jesus, the teacher and prophet, and so, throughout these pages, I will repeat these phrases from time to time.

Even had we lived and walked with Yeshua, whom we know as Jesus, we would not grasp him. No-one really knows the depths of any person, even those we have lived with intimately over thirty or forty years. So, when it comes to Jesus of Nazareth, at one level, we know very little for sure. In other ways, we know him as the living person at the centre of our faith.

A starting point for these reflections is that Jesus only makes sense if we understand him within his time and place and try to enter into his religious worldview: he was a faithful Jew immersed within Jewish culture and practices.

The Gospel accounts of Matthew, Mark, Luke and John are the remembered Jesus rather than the historical Jesus. This does not make them less 'true'. Each Gospel reflects its own understanding of the *meaning* of Jesus from the perspective of four different Christian communities solidified forty to seventy years after Jesus had been killed. Like Jesus, the earliest followers of Jesus were Jews and, initially, they were one amongst other Jewish sects at this time who were seeking ways to maintain their religious identity in a world dominated by the Romans.

The Gospels themselves emerged over decades as the early Christian communities reflected on their experience of Jesus; the oral tradition and preaching of the first disciples were passed on and ultimately began to be written down. The Gospels that resulted are theological statements about the meaning of Jesus. Chronology and historic details are less important than the insight and interpretation of a given evangelist writing for a particular community and its circumstances at that time. Each Gospel has its own purpose, audience, style and structure. Each needs to be read accordingly to grasp both its particular and more universal meaning. Its purpose was to inspire belief.

While I recognise the distinctive integrity of each Gospel, in this book, I deliberately draw threads from across all Gospels. There are obvious limitations in this approach.

Further, in seeking to comprehend what I cannot comprehend, I do so without the expertise of being a scripture scholar. I prepared for my travels and for my reflection upon the Gospels through selective reading that I hoped would inform and deepen my understanding of them. (Some of these are listed at the end of the book.) At the same time, I believe that the Gospels, and all sacred scripture, are there to be accessed by anyone who seeks the Word of God. They are not elitist documents only for scholars; inspired by the Spirit, the Gospels are a communication of God with the community and with me, inviting my response in word and action.

Approach

So this is not the work of a professional scripture scholar; it is not an exploration of the Gospels' design and literary shape; not an in-depth exploration of the history and land in which Jesus lived and died. It began as my attempt to express for myself my understanding, at this moment in my life, of the person Jesus. Given that Jesus taught in another language, from within another historical time and culture, the task is riddled with challenges. As in the Gospels themselves, in the following pages, I make no effort to follow a precise sequence of events (an impossible task anyway). The book is organised around themes with the simple intention – despite all the limitations – of exploring some sense of the sort of person Jesus was and the sort of things he did and how his observers and early followers perceived and understood him and his significance.[2]

How do we break open (as a friend likes to ask) the Gospel words? How do I get a little closer to understanding what this man was like to the people of his time? Understanding – even if just a little – how Jesus was perceived in his time helps me to relate to him now in my own time. And how to express what I discover? I was encouraged to follow my intuition to approach this reflection through a poetic medium when Brueggemann insists that 'when the text comes to speak about this alternative life wrought by God, the text must use poetry. There is no other way to speak...We know only enough to sing songs and speak poems... We stake our lives on such poems'.[3]

---

[2] To some extent, the themes around which the book are organised have been influenced by the comprehensive scholarly work of John P. Meier, *A Marginal Jew*, Volumes I-V, (see reading list.)

[3] Brueggemann, page 41.

The poetic form, tanka

My endeavour is to try to be as informed as I can about Jesus and then to use the language of poetry to express my highly subjective response.

I have chosen to work within the discipline of a literary and poetic form. Before there was the idea of a book, I began some reflections on Jesus using *tanka*, a short-form poetry genre with a long history. Tanka is a five-line form with origins in 8th or 9th century China and then Japanese court poetry.

Tanka's tight disciplined form offered restraint to my reflection. Tanka has certain attributes that seem appropriate to my purpose here: in its purest form it uses concrete images from everyday life and often juxtaposes two contrasting images that at first glance may not seem linked, but on reflection, one image adds insight into the other. There is often a 'pivot' line that can be read ('two-ways') for both images. This juxtaposition and shift from one image to another often carries a 'sting', an unexpected insight into the human condition that is implied (rather than bluntly stated). In fact, the best tanka are 'parables', told (in English) usually in less than thirty-one syllables with lots of space for 'dreaming' in their interpretation. Highly regarded tanka poet, Ishikawa Takuboku (1886–1912), called *tanka* 'poems made with both feet upon the ground... poems written without putting any distance from actual life'.[4] Because good poetry is always in touch with human life, it is very much of the spirit.

---

[4] Quoted in Amelia Fielden, 'About tanka and its history,' http://www.tankaonline.com/about. For more on tanka, see also http://www.tankasocietyofamerica.org/essays/what-is-tanka and http://www.eucalypt.info/E-articles.html

To illustrate this kind of poetry, here is a tanka that exemplifies the form.

> heart-deep in water
> past the gentle lap of waves
> into breaking surf –
> the breathlessness, the fear
> of loving one more time[5]

While my initial choice of tanka might have been somewhat intuitive, I was confirmed in my choice when I came across James Martin's chapter on parables in his *Jesus: A Pilgrimage*. 'The Greek *paraballō*', Martin writes, 'means "to place one thing beside another".' Martin, quoting Daniel Harrington, adds 'A parable is a form of analogy that seeks to illuminate one reality by appealing to something better known.'[6] Tanka uses metaphor rather than analogy, but just as stories can work their way into our imaginations, so do the images which are the tools of poetry. Parables can surprise, shock and scandalise; they are described as 'subversive': so too a good tanka with its twist and final lines.

Most, but not all, responses are in tanka form. In some instances, I have felt that the response was more appropriately expressed in prose or free verse.

'A good poem', writes Anne Thurston, 'refuses cheap grace and wrestles with the question which may or may not find its resolution'.[7] The poetry of this book may fail to satisfy such high expectations, but the process will be

---

[5] Carmel Summers, *Eucalypt*, Issue 20, 2016, page 3.
[6] James Martin, *Jesus, a pilgrimage*, HarperOne, New York, 2014, page 200, quoting Daniel Harrington SJ, *Jesus: a historical portrait*, St Anthony Messenger Press, Cincinnati, 2006, page 30.
[7] Anne Thurston, *A time of waiting: images and insights*, Columba Press, Dublin, 2004, page 16.

in a language that, I hope, touches the spirit because this particular pilgrimage is one of the spirit and its language should be that of image.

Overview

Each chapter is organised around a theme, with several sub-sections.

Each chapter, and most sections, tries to weave together four components:

i. scripture references pertinent to the theme, mostly from the Gospels but also from the Hebrew scriptures where appropriate;
ii. brief notes on the context for the readings and the place/s where the specific Gospel incidence might have occurred;
iii. responses to the scripture and reflections for prayer;
iv. quotations at the end of each chapter for those interested in additional insights and reading.

Using the book

I began this as a very personal search. In the process, it occurred to me that others might also find it useful for reflection, enquiry and prayer. This could include parish groups, pastoral councils, staff groups, leadership teams or individuals for their own purposes.

The starting point in each chapter is the selection of readings from scripture. These scriptural references are an essential element of reading the book. The responses and reflections that follow in each section draw on these readings and are informed by them.

The reflections are intended to be taken in small bites... they are intended more as a tapas plate than a full-course meal. Groups might choose to read (silently and aloud), reflect and then share some aspect of the reflection, not as a discussion, but as a personal response to be shared with others in an atmosphere of trust that is conducive to individual or shared prayer. Sometimes, it will be simpler to start with just some of the readings listed and to return to the others later.

One way to use the book would be to space the 11 chapters over the year, allocating one of the 55 sub-sections per week. In this way, the scripture passages can be enjoyed over the course of a given week, slowly and selectively.

There are various approaches to entering the scripture passages that many people would be familiar with, involving silent reading, or spoken reading, in each case allowing time for silence and a re-reading of the text.[8]

One very accessible way of praying with the scriptures is the traditional approach known as *lectio divina*.[9] This traditional form of meditation is premised on us opening ourselves to receive the Word and letting God's word speak to us.

---

[8] There are many resources available to assist individuals and groups in prayerful reflection on the scriptures. One that I have found helpful is *The Gospels for Prayer*. Michael Hansen SJ (Editor) *The Gospels for Prayer*, Ave Maria Press, Notre Dame, Indiana, 2003.

[9] For descriptions of *Lectio divina*, see https://www.loyolapress.com/catholic-resources/prayer/personal-prayer-life/different-ways-to-pray/lectio-divina/ or ACBC, 'Lectio Divina' in Catholic Australia \setup [url]\hyphenatedurl {https://www.catholicaustralia.com.au/the-scripture/lectio-divina}

In preparing to read and pray the scriptures, we can draw inspiration and learn from *Dadirri*, the 'deep listening' taught by Miriam-Rose Ungunmerr-Baumann.[10]

If these reflections help you to reflect upon Jesus, then that is enough.

Something to think about

After decades of study exploring the historical Jesus, John Meier concluded: 'The more we understand Jesus in his own time and place, the more alien he will seem to us'.[11]

*

'No one's Jesus and no one Jesus suits everyone.'[12]

*

'... the Christian concept of *logos* is also poetic no less than philosophical. And one finds much more poetry than philosophy in the Bible... Poetic language is not about the certainty of dogmatic orthodoxy. Such certainty does not bring one salvation.'[13]

*

---

[10] See Miriam-Rose Ungunmerr, https://www.miriamrosefoundation.org.au/dadirri/

[11] John Meier (referencing Albert Schweitzer) in *The Marginal Jew*, Vol I, page 200.

[12] Meier, Vol I, page 3.

[13] Massimo Faggioli, *The Church in a change of era. How the Franciscan reforms are changing the Catholic Church*, La Croix International, E-book, 2019, pages 3-4, https://international.la-croix.com/uploads/the-church-in-a-change-of-era/the-church-in-a-change-of-era.pdf

Brueggemann asserts that it takes 'poets that speak against a prose world' to lead us to a 'life unclosed, life made open, certitude broken so that we can re-decide, images moving, imagination assaulting ideology' so that we can speak of meaning to our 'prose-flattened world'.[14]

---

[14] Brueggemann, *Finally comes the poet*, Introduction.

1
Prelude

Mural in the Basilica of the Nativity, Bethlehem

1.1 A certain place in time

Reading

Genesis 22

On my first day in Israel, I am taken with our group to Abraham's lookout, high above Jerusalem. The land of the Abrahamic scriptures sprawls before us: the Kidron Valley, down which Jesus and his friends walked on the way to Gethsemane, passes by tombs already cut into the valley walls; the now-green valley of Ben-Hinnom on the southern border of ancient Jerusalem where it is said that pagans once sacrificed their children in the fires of Gehenna and where outcasts were buried; the dark green shadows of the distant Mount of Olives. These are places associated with patriarchs, prophets and kings; with struggle and victories; with 4,000 years of documented events from Abraham to the present.

Dominating everything is the golden Dome of the Rock above the site of the Second temple, contested holy ground for Jews and Muslims. The magnificent shrine, which is the Dome of the Rock, was constructed between 688-691 CE as a Muslim 'noble sanctuary'. Nearby is the Al Aqsa Mosque constructed between 705-715 CE. The Dome of the Rock was built in line with the Byzantine Resurrection Basilica and in harmony with its design.[15] The Dome of the Rock honoured the story of the 'Night Journey', the journey made by the Prophet Muhammad from the Great Mosque in Mecca to the Temple Mount in Jerusalem. Here, the Prophet led Abraham, Moses, Jesus and other prophets in prayer before his ascension into heaven. Jerusalem holds a special place as a holy city for Muslims. Jerusalem was captured by the Knights Templar in 1099 and the Dome of the Rock converted for use as a church before being reclaimed as a Muslim site early in the 12th Century CE.

---

[15] Dr Jutta Sperber, 'How Jerusalem became holy in Islam', lecture given at Tantur Ecumenical Institute, 12 July 2018.

The tension between Muslims and Israeli police which erupts regularly around the Dome of the Rock on Fridays in our times has a long history, given that the Dome of the Rock and the Al Aqsa Mosque are built on the holiest site in the Jewish faith – the site of the Second Jewish Temple, with the Mosque being constructed over what was the temple courtyard.

So much history has unfolded in such a small area of land. Sacred space, it hits me, can be a place of intensity. *Terra sancta.*

What makes somewhere *holy* ground? Did it seem that way to Abraham? To Isaac? How mindful of this was the young woman from Nazareth as she travelled to visit her cousin Elizabeth? It clearly was holy ground for John the Baptiser who grew to become determined and visionary? 'Holiness is non-rational', one scholar observed. 'Theology rationalises it.'[16]

Our group is given a small glimpse of the point in history when Jesus was born when we travel to the West Bank. Our guide takes us to Herodium, about twelves kilometres south of Jerusalem. Herod, of Jewish background, was appointed by the Romans to rule over the people of Judah. Here, on an artificial mountain, the man known as King Herod the Great (or King Herod the Horrible from another perspective), built a lavish, multi-storey fortress palace, replete with baths, banquet rooms and a Roman theatre. Now only ruins remain.

Amongst eroded columns, steps and rock walls on the lower reaches of the hill, we listen to the history of Herod's murderous rule of the Jewish people. On rocks dating back two thousand years, we watch goat kids gambol, herded by

---

[16] Dr Jutta Sperber

young Palestinian boys, who in turn are watched over by an adult male, mobile phone to his ear. This was Herod's summer fortress-residence, complete with a colonnaded pool on which he sailed boats.

> a mountain
> fortress of power
> built on fear –
> only fallen rocks remain
> and the yammer of young goats

1.2 A young woman in Nazareth

Reading

Jeremiah 23:5-6, 2 Samuel 7:12-16, Luke 1:26-38, 3:23b-38, Matthew 1

Place

Nazareth in Galilee (according to Luke). Modern Nazareth is a congested commercial centre with a population of around 80,000. It is dry and hot in summer – 38 degrees on the days I was there. The area, in the foothills of Israel's northern region of Galilee, is fertile with an abundance of wheat, grapes, figs, peaches, almonds and palms. The heavy use of water comes at a high cost to the water table.

In 4BCE Nazareth, families lived in kinship groups either in caves or in simple stone homes with woven roofs. Most families probably shared the space with their animals.

Beneath the convent where I stayed in 2018, an Italian sister showed us excavations of small dwellings with low entrances and interconnected rooms. Life in these homes, with their narrow connecting alleyways, would have been close and intimate.

Context

Matthew's Gospel opens with a bold declaration of faith in Jesus as Messiah. This Gospel is at pains to show that Joseph is descended from the royal house of David. (Luke's Gospel, on the other hand, written for converts of Greek background, traces Jesus' lineage back to Adam.) Matthew reports how the mother of Jesus was betrothed to Joseph, who accepted the child as his own. Joseph's legal acceptance of Jesus as his son confers on Jesus hereditary rights of messianic lineage.

Francis Moloney points out that the messianic lineage traced in Matthew's Gospel includes the names of five women. Because this is most unusual for such genealogies in the Hebrew scriptures and contemporary cultures, it indicates – Moloney argues – that Matthew wished deliberately to highlight the role of women as 'wonderful instruments of God's plan' because of their being 'open to God's action in their lives, cost them what it may'. Thus, Matthew's genealogy of the Messiah of Israel reaches its fruition in the young woman of Nazareth who became the mother of 'Jesus' whose name means 'saviour'.[17]

1.2a. Unexpected

She is young, living in a hamlet of a few hundred people. She knows little about the world beyond that out-of-the-way village. Something breaks into her life, disturbing the predictable pattern of her days. She senses herself addressed, as in the Greek Orthodox *Akathistos* hymn, *Hail, Space for the uncontained God... Rejoice, Receptacle of the Wisdom of God... Rejoice, Assurance of those who pray in silence.*[18]

>   someone calls me
>   speaking of things
>   that cannot be
>   confusing me
>   surely, with someone else

Yet the familiar is there too in the language of the messenger: a young woman, raised in the faith of her family and that of her ancestors, knows she belongs to the people of God. She knows of God's promises, knows the man she is betrothed to marry is descended from the House of David.

>   outside
>   sunlight quivers
>   a lamb bleats
> piercing the stillness
>   inside her room

---

[17] Francis J. Moloney, SDB, *Woman: first among the faithful*, Dove Communications, Melbourne, 1984, pages 33-37.
[18] Taken from Greek Orthodox Akathistos hymn, eg, https://www.youtube.com/watch?v=K2IYzQ2Ava4

Do not be afraid. Your son will be called 'Yeshua', the rescuer. This last, simple enough for her to understand: a blessing from the Lord God, her child will be a life saver.

> held in stasis
> before she answers,
> the world turns
> on its axis, her life
> in its trajectory

And, the poet writes, 'God waited'.[19]
Then the young girl Miryam says, 'Yes. Amen. As God wishes'. Yes, to a future she cannot know. And if she knew...

> *Yes*, she says
> to the unexpected,
> the unborn,
> the unknown, embraced
> with each new mother's *yes*

Aren't there 'annunciations of one sort or another in all our lives?'[20]

1.2b. Miryam's journey

Reading

Luke 1:39

---

[19] Adapted from Denise Levertov, 'Annunciation', quoted by C. Page in https://inaspaciousplace.wordpress.com/2012/12/12/annunciation/
[20] Ibid.

Place

The hill country of Judea is in the south of Israel, down near Jerusalem. It would take about six days to travel by foot from Nazareth. A young woman would not have made this journey alone. She would have travelled in the company of known people.

Context

Luke's Gospel focuses on the two children in the women's wombs – the first meeting between John and Jesus – and John's embryonic leap of recognition of who Jesus is. Her unborn child's movement surprises Elizabeth to cry out with wonder and joy. The reflection below focuses on the two women, both pregnant with godly design.

Travelling

She leaves the familiarity of her home to travel to her relative,

> the water vessel
> fresh-filled, chills
> her skin
> trembling… expectant
> and uncertain

In the caravan, she keeps to herself, practising the words she will use to tell the older woman.

> on her lips
> songs her mother sang
> of steadfast love –
> she lets
> mystery unfold

1.3 Ein Kerem

Reading

Exodus 15, 1 Samuel 2:1-10, Psalm 34, Psalm 103, Luke 1:39-56

Place

The village of Ein Kerem is a drive of about ten kilometres southwest from the centre of Jerusalem through pleasantly treed hills. Beyond the cluster of coffee shops and the lanes of tourist stalls, the Church of St John the Baptiser marks John's reported birthplace. Geraniums blaze red in the sunshine. The name of the village is said to mean 'spring of the vineyard'.

Context

In this song attributed to Miryam, Luke is referencing both the previously childless Hannah, who gave birth to the prophet Samuel; and Miriam, sister of Moses. In John Rutter's version of the *Magnificat* with the Cambridge Singers, one can easily imagine the two women swirling and swooping with joy around the kitchen fire as they sing together their chorus to God's love.

1.3a. Women together

Miryam comes to the home of Elizabeth. The young woman has come to support her older relative in her unexpected late pregnancy. They greet each other with affection.

> my body thrills
> to have you here with me
> in the kitchen
> sitting by the fire
> savouring chatter

Elizabeth recognises immediately what the younger woman has not acknowledged: she sees that Miryam too is pregnant.

They spend time together: two women, surprised by pregnancy. Each cares for the other, old for young and young for old, until Elizabeth's boy is born. Over these three months, there is time, in their domesticity, to ponder the things that each is experiencing. 'If we've heard correctly', they might have said, 'then God *does* favour the weak and side with the poor. It is incomprehensible – and amazing – that he is acting through us simple ones, and women at that'.

> this is a song
> I will sing to my child –
> how the most holy
> the Almighty listens
> to those of no consequence

> this is a song
> I will sing to my child –
> how God loves
> the simple-hearted
> who strive to be faithful
>
> this is a song
> I will sing to my child –
> how in the night
> afraid and lonely
> I am comforted
>
> this is a song
> I will sing to my child –
> how God's word
> within me wells up,
> spills over with joy

Two new mothers imagine what their children will become: Elizabeth's son, son of a priest, would hear God's voice call him away from the temple to the desert, to a life of austerity, fearless critic and fiery prophet. Miryam's son would hear God's voice call him to the margins, to a life of drinking and eating with sinners, parable weaver, bearing the news of God's love. Both would proclaim God's kingdom; both would attract disciples; both would die as young men.

Elizabeth's son beheaded in a palace prison cell; Miryam's son hung outside the walls.

1.3b. Returning home

In Ein Kerem, Miryam could begin to marvel how her body was changing. She leaves Elizabeth, walking with the gravitas of a life-bearer.

> by the road
> pomegranates and figs
> swell with summer –
> each day her body
> pulses with creation

What first-time mother knows what to expect? Books can give some insights. Elders can advise. But each new life makes its presence known in a woman's flesh, in silent messages between what we once knew as our bodies and what they are becoming.

Becoming a mother is to face the strange and new and wonderful. Exciting and fearful. Fulfilling and frightening. How will she explain this to Joseph and her family?

Yet the angel had promised Miryam that the shadow of the Most High would enfold her.

> within the shelter
> of her family's faith
> she, in turn,
> enfolds her unborn
> in the sanctuary of her womb

1.4 Bethlehem

1.4a. Shepherds' Field

Reading

Ruth 4, I Samuel 16:1-13, Micah 5, Luke 2:1-20, Matthew 2, John 7:42

Place

Bethlehem, separated from Jerusalem by an ugly wall, is built on steep slopes that are stony and hard underfoot. In some places, the hills have been terraced with limestone. Afternoon sun bakes them and hazes the distant slopes. They are thirsty hillsides, yet the abundance of sage green olives contradicts the parched sense of the place in summer. Underfoot, unpaved roads are flint-hard and dusty.

Context

Some scholars suggest that Jesus was not necessarily born in Bethlehem, and more likely in Nazareth. Because of its association with David, however, Bethlehem served a theological purpose for the early Christians reflecting on the meaning of their experience of Jesus. Bethlehem continues to hold a sacred place in the Jesus story.

Response

On the outskirts of Bethlehem are the Fields of Boaz (where Ruth gleaned after harvest) and Shepherds' Fields. This was the ancestral home of the House of David from whom it was written the Messiah would come: Ruth's son became the father of Jesse; Jesse became the father of David; David was the shepherd boy anointed by Samuel to be king.

Limestone caves are still visible along the edges of the valleys here. These are the homes where ancient shepherds lived, sheltering with their families, their flocks kept safe in winter towards the rear of the caves. Near the entrance of one such cave, the pale stone roof is blackened by cooking fires and oil-lamp smoke.

> no space in an inn
> but a cousin's cousin
> welcomes us
> and give us privacy
> warm with the breath of beasts
>
> in the quiet
> of Shepherd's Field,
> a hearth holds space
> for travellers
> heavy with expectancy
>
> news of a baby
> brings curious visitors
> neighbours abuzz,
> shepherd-kin return home
> alight with stars and signs
>
> the kettle hisses,
> tea is poured,
> the child's lineage
> is scrutinised...
> royal house of David

1.4b. New mother

Reading

Luke 2:1-39, especially verse 19

I love this child
so much it seems
my heart has space
for no-one other
yet it does – wondrously

my eyelids scratch
with sands of sleeplessness,
my breasts ache
with a surge of milk –
I am stilled in awe

he sleeps
warm against me
helpless, soft trusting
hopes I dare to hold
prickle with fear

as he nuzzles
tiny fingers curl around
everything I know
each moment after this
is an act of letting go

1.4c. Star-Seekers

Reading

Matthew 2:1-12

A Magi's Response

I saw it first one cold solitary night. Solitude, signs and stars: the tools of our priestly caste. Not all the magi were convinced, but I had checked the charts and prophecies and tracked this *stella nova*'s passage over many months through the heavens, heading west.

After careful preparations, we are under way. Persepolis now a memory – who knows when I will see its cedar-columned halls again? We are ready for as many lunar cycles as needs to reach this star's zenith: supplies and handpicked cameleers, woodsmen, huntsmen. In our caravan a dozen of the wisest in astronomy and meanings – sages from India, Arabia and Persia; and, yes, a Hebrew versed in their belief in a Messiah. He could be useful.

> weevils in the grain
> the smell of sheep and camels
> day after day
> journeying
> becomes my life

We travel mostly by the moon, hiding from the sun in sleep. The old men find it hard and go slowly. Winter nights are cruel. Sand in our eyes abrades the sharp certainty of our vision. Tomorrow's dawn will shine on yet another sea of sand, with wave after wave of ridges still to cross. This morning, we crested a rugged peak, only to see before us the tracks we had made some two nights ago. Some in our group begin to doubt the wisdom of our search. Let them turn back.

> thick cloud
> for days now
> lost
> in the folly
> of a dream

We come into the territory of the king, Herod. We seek him out and pay respects. He calls his priests to point out the hamlet where their prophets say the new king will be born. He gets his men to ply us with refreshments and cheers us in our quest. I find this welcome comfort, for we are now worn ragged by our travails. 'Come back, report to me', he says.

We find the house, no different from any other: a young woman doing homely chores; her child burbling sweet nonsense.

> for so long
> so far, we gave our lives
> to this star
> in search of Wisdom
> we find only a child

The Hebrew is in a trance of happiness. I hear him in his tent at night chanting

> *I search for you*
> *from dawn and long for you*
> *to see your might*
> *my mouth sings praise to you*
> *my heart rejoices*

The locals in the shabby town avoid us. Not just because we are from the East, but they have heard we talked to

Herod. Their hated king. We shall not return to Herod when we leave; we will go another way.

Something to think about

Mary's 'greatness lies in the fact that she is, above all, a woman of faith. The girl from Nazareth could not possibly be expected to understand the depths of the mystery that was being revealed to her, a mystery in which she was to play an indispensable role: the giver of the flesh and blood in the mystery of the Incarnation. How all this could be, and why it should happen to her, she could not understand; but as mother of all believers – of all of us caught up in the same wonderful mystery of God's ways in our lives – ... she 'treasured all these things and pondered over them in her heart'. (Luke 2:19, 51)[21]

*

'What can we do to make it clear to all – the women themselves, as well as the men who dominate the Christian Church – that we have remythologised women? The study of the sources of our faith indicates that we must repeat in our own age what Jesus of Nazareth and the early Church seem to have done: a demythologisation. In the New Testament, woman is clearly first in time and quality in the order of faith, and thus she assumes a leadership role in man's search for faith.'[22]

*

'Jesus called for a discipleship of equals that still needs to be discovered and realised by women and men today.'[23]

---

[21] Moloney, *Woman*, page 53.
[22] Moloney, *Woman*, page 94.
[23] Elizabeth Schüssler Fiorenza, In memory of her, SCM Press, London, page 154.

2

Early life, pre-ministry

Mother and Child, Milk Grotto, Bethlehem

2.1 Yeshua of Nazareth

Reading

Luke 2:39, Matthew 2:19-23

Place

Generally, the people of 1st century Nazareth were poor. Many were indigent, sick, widowed, homeless and landless peasants. People worked in the fields of those who owned land, in addition to the chores of daily survival: weaving, grinding, planting, baking, caring for animals. Nazareth was a backwater place that city people would ridicule, 'Can any good come from Nazareth?'

Context

The Romans occupied Israel and controlled the provinces through local rulers who needed to prove – often through violence – their value to their foreign masters. Herod, known as 'the Great', a Roman-appointed ruler, was a man of extraordinary cruelty.

Herod died in 4 BCE when Jesus was just a toddler. His death led to uprisings from the local people including an attack on Sepphoris, a city just six kilometres from Nazareth. In 3BCE, soldiers of the Roman Governor of Syria, Varus, burned Sepphoris and razed the surrounding villages, beheading the villagers or taking them as slaves. During Jesus' childhood, hundreds of peasants who had revolted were crucified along the roadway between Nazareth and Capernaum. Around 2,000 Jews were taken from Galilee and crucified near Jerusalem.

After Herod's death, the country's regions were shared among his sons, with Herod Antipas becoming the Tetrarch of Galilee. It was a more peaceful time, although Antipas would later order the murder of John the Baptiser.

Although we know very little about the early life of Jesus, it is understood that his family would have been part of the hard-working poor. He would have observed at close hand many who were desperately poor, 'marginal people who lived their lives of quiet desperation'.

2.1a Lives of quiet desperation[24]

> Who are these men who rule us,
> grind our heartache into our sweat?
> Take our bread before it's baked,
> snatch the grapes we watch and water,
> trample the vines of our existence?
> They say they serve our god
> yet they pay their primary homage
> unto Caesar.
>
> At night before they sleep, our children
> hear us elders talk in whispers
> under woven palm leaves: how
> someone heard, on pilgrimage,
> that forty-two young men of ours
> were burned alive. And of corpses
> stinking on their crosses on the road
> to Capernaum.
>
> This land, our land, so reverently
> tended by our fathers walking gently,
> as they planted out their seed and hungers:
> and she gave figs and wheat and hope.

---

[24] Frank Andersen msc, *Jesus our story*, HarperCollinsReligious, Melbourne, 2001 edition, page 15.

2.1b Palestinian village, West Bank 2012

The village is approached from a side road off the main highway. Hard stones on the roadway, low stone walls supporting terraces. Some homes are built from cement blocks. Some are poor, some quite elegant, some demolished.

In 2012, there was still no running water coming into the village although the infrastructure is ready. The electricity supply is recent, with the villagers providing all the poles. There is a school built by the village men and women. The children are walked to school under the protection of adults, and, because of the isolation and danger, all teachers are male.

Jewish settlers from a nearby ridge keep extending into the fields traditionally owned by the village. They have planted peach trees and barley and have destroyed a fence of steel spikes and barbed wire that the villagers had constructed to protect their land.

Resistance typifies this outpost, resistance hard as flint: resistance against all odds of eking a livelihood from the rocky slopes, resistance to the ingression of settlers, and the settlers' own resistance to another way.

2.2 Jesus and his family

Reading

Isaiah 11:1, Isaiah 60, Luke 2:39-51, 4:16, John 1:46

Place

About the early life of Jesus one thing is certain: very little is certain.

Context

Jesus of Nazareth was born sometime between 7BCE and 4 BCE to a young woman in her mid-teens known in Hebrew as Miryam and in Aramaic as Maryam, and a man called Joseph who was regarded as his father. His name was *Yeshua* (from *Yesoshua* meaning *The Lord saves*). The Gospels and Acts of the Apostles in various places refer to the 'brothers of Jesus' – James, Joses, Jude and Simon – and unnamed 'sisters', all possibly stepsiblings or cousins.

The family were Palestinian Jews living in Galilee and speaking Aramaic. They were poor and respectable, in the way of most of their neighbours in Nazareth; they were not destitute, and probably didn't live in a cave as many did but with extended family in a cluster of small adobe dwellings.

While Joseph has traditionally been thought of as a woodworker, it is possible that he worked in stone as it was the most common material available. It is likely that, from around the age of twelve, Jesus worked with him, as well as being involved in some agricultural work. Some scholars suggest it is possible that, in their search for work, Jesus and his father worked on the re-building of the city of Sepphoris.

2.2a His place

It is early morning on a rocky outcrop of a hill towering over a vast valley near Nazareth. In these first days of May, the wind is crisp. The sun gradually warms the large flat rocks on which I sit. Wildflowers toss orange, pink and blue heads among the grasses. Mount Tabor stands out above the plains to the east; the Mediterranean, less than fifty kilometres to the west, is hidden by fog.

>amongst the rocks
>boys play and chase
>wildflowers in the wind
>red hollyhocks a child
>might gather for his mum

Far below lies the Valley of Jezreel. It is verdant with cultivation: fish farms, vineyards, green tracts and peach orchards. The hum of machinery, the whirr of tyres on a highway, the crowing of roosters drifts up the steep valley wall. A ten-year-old, who'd heard his people's stories, might hear sounds of ancient battles, shield against shield, screams of betrayal, the groans of Armageddon.

>from Mount Tabor
>ten thousand men on foot
>charge Canaans
>chariots bog in mud
>be-fouled with blood

The prophet Hosea wrote of this valley, Jezreel, when he compared the House of Judah to his own unfaithful wife. Here Joseph lived a goodly life, with his wife and their family, in expectation that the promised Messiah would emerge from within their community, descended as they were from the line of David. Here, Jesus learns practical skills from Joseph.

> hands guide
> a boy's small hands
> to plane and craft –
> from a tree cut down
> the stump puts out a shoot[25]

A road cuts across the valley below where I sit. It heads south towards Jerusalem, about 150 kilometres, a week's walk. Did the young boy Yeshua sit on these same rocks, facing Jerusalem? When did he realise he would one day have to broach its crowds, threats and city scape?

> no thunder
> on the mountain side
> this morning
> only quiet in my heart
> and a murmuring breeze[26]

2.3 About God

Reading

Isaiah 11:1, Nehemiah 9, Jeremiah 31:1-3

---

[25] Cf. Isaiah 11:1.
[26] Cf. 1 Kings 19:11-13.

Place

Israel was a religious society. It was a nation of believers whose identity was shaped by the covenant, the intervention of God in their history: their deliverance from slavery in Egypt, defeats in war, and their subsequent exile to Babylon. Throughout all of this, God was understood to be Israel's friend, the transcendent God who had their interests at heart.

By the first century of the Common Era (CE), some Jewish religious leaders (as happens with all religious groups) emphasised the observance of the law, ritual and religious practices at the expense of the spirit of true worship. At the same time, Judaism in the first century was complex and multi-layered, lived out under foreign rule.

Context

It has been suggested that Nazareth was part of a religious awakening of Jewish national and religious identity when a group, who considered themselves descendants of King David, settled in a deserted village as immigrants from the Babylonian exile, sometime in the 1-2 century BCE. These returning exiles called themselves *Nazoreans*. 'A shoot shall come out from the stump of Jesse, and a branch (*nezer*) shall grow out of his roots' (Isaiah 11:1).

Prayers and blessings are an integral element in the days of practising Jewish women and men. In the heightened religious observance of his native place, Jesus would have been immersed in the practice of daily prayer (at set times), rituals of food and washing, observance of the Sabbath and the overall religious character of his society.

His family would have observed the three key festivals of *Pesah* or Passover (the spring Feast of Unleavened Bread commemorating God's liberation of the Israelites from slavery in Egypt), *Shavuot* or Pentecost (the Feast of Weeks, commemorating the giving of the Law – Torah – at Mount Sinai) and *Sukkot* (the Feast of Tents commemorating harvest and the Israelites' leaving Egypt) by making pilgrimage to the temple.

Most importantly, his religious immersion shaped the path he would take away from Nazareth.

2.3a The problem of God

I have loved you with an everlasting love... I remember precisely the moment when I heard those words. I remember the year, the building, the room where I was sitting, the others with me, listening to a lecture on scripture: *I have loved you with an everlasting love...* Like a bolt from the blue, like a defibrillator to my heart, this was God speaking to me in a way I had not heard before. Speaking to *me*.

It wasn't as though that moment settled all my 'god' questions for the rest of my life. Later as a university student and then on through my life, I have kept returning to 'who is God?' That overwhelming moment of clarity, however, has anchored the way I face those questions. Ultimately, I have chosen again and again to see my life within that perspective: I choose to live within a worldview that orients life within the providence of a loving, living God who is both transcendent and immanent.

I was only at the beginning of my research for this book when it hit me forcibly that Jesus only makes sense within the context of his relationship with God, within a society shaped by its religious worldview and history. Jesus was a faithful observant Jew. Jesus only matters and only makes sense (in so far as he does make sense) if one has a sense of God, a sense of the divine.

This strikes me as one of the biggest challenges for a contemporary westerner of the 21st Century in trying to understand Jesus of Nazareth a little better: *God.* Who is God? This is not easily answered in western contemporary contexts which hold secularism and divergent religious practices in tension. The pioneer Swiss psychologist, Carl Jung, famously had carved over his door, *Called or not, God is present.* Such a statement might provoke a 'so what' shrug of shoulders from many people today.

In the first place, some of us have been nurtured in narrow, artificial, unimaginative ideas of God, some modelled on our worst rule-makers, judges and parents. I say, alleluia, when modern society rejects that view of God. There are alternative understandings of the divine, of course, understandings that are always in process, always unfolding, as we search for the incomprehensible, following our human instinct for the infinite. While human nature might be 'the grammar of God's self-utterance,' (as Karl Rahner wrote),[27] this is not without its ambivalence, and it sometimes seems too easy to hanker for a nostalgic reclamation, a reinstallation of a surer God, even one that verges on the superstitious and who is almost anti-incarnational.

---

[27] Karl Rahner, *Foundations of Christian Faith*, Seabury, New York, 1978, quoted in Elizabeth Johnson csj and Susan Rakoczy ihm, *Who do you say that I am?* Cluster Publications, Pietermaritzburg, 1997, page 21.

For our purposes here, I decided to focus on one part of the 'God problem' through this question: who was the God of 1st century Jews in Nazareth?

2.3b Kaleidoscope of infinity

Drawing inspiration from the Jewish practice of prayer and blessings, the following section attempts to reflect some of the images and names God that might have been familiar to an observant Jewish person in first century CE and to re-present them in more contemporary language. I am very aware of the limitations in this reflection.

Blessed are you, O Lord,
God of Abraham, God of Isaac and God of Jacob...

summer sunlight
glitters on the ocean
your power shimmers
in the majesty of stars
moons, planets and the cosmos[28]

You mould
mountains into shape,
carve out desert wastes
when you breathe
each blade of grass trembles[29]

You take pleasure
in showing mercy
over and over
You fling our failings
to the bottom of the sea[30]

---

[28] Isaiah 40:12-ff.
[29] Psalm 8, Psalm 104, Psalm 148.
[30] Psalm 86:15-16, Psalm 103, Hosea 14, Psalm 51, Micah 7:18-19, Psalm 145.

love is your name –
steadfast flame
constant ocean
tender bride and groom
faithful mum and dad[31]

holy God
greater than your power
is the mystery
of all that is sacred
...and so close[32]

our Lifesaver
always faithful
to your agreement
constant in rescuing
your people with justice[33]

I trip
and fall down in a heap
again and again
you hold out a helping hand
a patient listening ear[34]

You listen
to the grief of the poor
You call out
for the homeless, the weak,
the abused, the tyrannised[35]

You are the way
to soft-spoken Wisdom
so trustworthy

---

[31] Psalm 89, 115
[32] Isaiah 40:25.
[33] Psalm 114, 105, Exodus 3:13.
[34] Nehemiah 9:17.
[35] Isaiah 42, Psalm 72, Psalm 41.

even simpletons
like me can find her[36]

You bend down
to listen to my sighs
brushing close
to gather my tears
into your hand[37]

driven from my home
lamenting lost children
I'm covered in shame –
you find me asylum,
I learn to sing with gladness[38]

when we are weary
you carry us as lambs
leading mother ewes
to rest secure
beside running water[39]

the earth shakes loose
a tsunami of disaster
is upon me –
you are Gibraltar,
an Uluru at my back[40]

my plans for myself
are chaff dust –
you are an eagle
carrying me to heights
I could not imagine[41]

---

[36] Psalm 19, Job 28, Proverbs 8.
[37] Psalm 56, Psalm 116.
[38] Jeremiah 31, Psalm 100.
[39] Isaiah 40:10-11, Psalm 23.
[40] Psalm 18, 91:1-2.
[41] Deuteronomy 32:11-12, Hosea 13:8.

as a mother,
you teach me how to walk,
kiss my grazed knees,
comfort my broken heart:
we are tied with cords of love[42]

You knew me
when I was in the womb,
you nursed me
at your breast.
you will not forget me[43]

like a woman
groaning and gasping
in labour
you bring us,
your people, into life[44]

You protect us
from unseen danger –
chickens hidden
from wild birds and foxes
beneath a mother hen's wings[45]

You rejoice
in those who hope in you –
those who hope in you
fall asleep singing,
wake up full of smiles[46]

*Blessed are you, O Lord,
God of Abraham, God of Isaac and God of Jacob...*[47]

---

[42] Isaiah 66:13, Hosea 11.
[43] Isaiah 49:15, Psalm 131:2.
[44] Isaiah 42:14.
[45] Psalm 17:8, Psalm 57:1-2, Psalm 91, Matthew 23:37; Luke 13:34.
[46] Psalm 4, Psalm 33, Psalm 34, Psalm 92.
[47] Traditional Jewish prayer and blessing.

2.4 Bringing up the lad

Reading

Exodus: 28:1-3, Deuteronomy 12:11, Psalm 24, Psalm 48, Psalm 26:8, Psalm 100, Isaiah 2:3, 24:23, Matthew 1:16-24, Luke 2:41-51

Place

Through their decades in the wilderness, the Israelites carried with them the symbol of the Covenant in the portable tabernacle known as the Ark of the Covenant. At Mount Sinai, they were instructed to seek out the special place for honouring this covenant – the Promised Land. King David set up his capital in Jerusalem, and around 1000 BCE, his son Solomon built the first temple there on Mount Zion. And here the Ark of the Covenant was placed, in the Holy of Holies, the reminder of God's covenant with the Israelites.

In 587 BCE, the Babylonians destroyed the Temple of Solomon and the Second Temple was completed around 538 BCE. This temple was significantly extended by Herod the Great around 20 BCE. And it is to this newly restored and expanded Second Temple that Jesus and his parents would have made their pilgrimages.

The Second Temple was destroyed by the Romans in 70 CE, around forty years after the death of Jesus and around the time that the Gospel of Mark was written.

Context

The Hebrew scriptures describe the rituals and services conducted in the temple. Daily offerings of animals, pigeons, cereal or liquids were made, with special sacrifices on the Sabbath and during festivals, performed by priests on behalf of the faithful. Aaron became the first priest, charged with the duty of offering sacrifices according to the law given to Moses; and all priests were descendants of the tribe of Levi, to which Moses and his brother Aaron belonged. (Zechariah, the father of John the Baptiser, was a Levitical priest.)

The temple was a place of worship and prayer for individuals and where the traditional prayers that are still used today, such as the *Shema*, were recited. Psalms were sung by the priests during the daily offerings, with different psalms for each day of the week.

Scholars agree that Jesus probably experienced an intense religious education at home, and that he was probably literate. He would have learnt the scriptures, memorising them 'by heart'. He might have received some education in the local synagogue and he probably had some knowledge of Hebrew, especially from reading biblical Hebrew as part of his upbringing. While his everyday language was Aramaic, given the linguistic diversity of Galilee, he possibly also knew some Greek.

Debates about interpretations of Law (the Torah) were common among teachers and religious leaders at the time. Apparently, Jesus developed a good knowledge of scriptures that he would use later in his teaching and discussions with the other religious leaders. Perhaps, even as a child, he observed groups discussing details of the Law in his own synagogue. When he was twelve, he went with his family as usual to Jerusalem to celebrate the Passover festival.

2.4a 'Within your gates'[48]

We've tried to raise him in the tradition, teaching him our observances. Each year, we travel to Jerusalem for the festivals. He is already familiar with the journey and the rituals and we are all excited as we prepare for the journey for this Passover. He is growing. Now he is twelve, it is more important that he understands.

Afterwards, on our way home, we realise he is not with us. An awkward age. I was thinking he was with his mum; she thought he was with me. Already, we've spent one full day on the road back home

We go from group to group, expecting to find him. He knew we had to leave; knew when we were leaving. He's big enough to know better. His mother is distraught, imagining the worst, dangers on the road and in the city. I've watched this boy. He's too smart to be conned by someone. I'm more annoyed than anything. What does he think he is up to? His mother doesn't need this anxiety.

After a sleepless night, we leave before it's fully light, tagging ourselves onto a group that's on their way to the city. That night, when we reach the city gate, we go to the lodgings we had used. No sight of him. His mother and I sit all night, not a wink of sleep. All next day, we roam around the streets, going to markets and back to the lodgings in case he returns. Asking, asking, had anyone seen a boy of twelve. Of course, they have, lots of them. Jerusalem is full of young boys, running and walking, talking with friends, playing

---
[48] Psalm 122.

games and doing errands. Another long night, waiting and praying. We keep asking ourselves what he had said to us in the last few days, what we had said to him, why would he go off like this, who he might he be with, what kind of people, where is he sleeping, what is he eating.

It's three days before we find him. Can you imagine how his mother's been? That morning we go to the temple. Such a vast and bustling place, although not as crowded now the festival has passed. Again, we ask. Then we see him, with a group of elders. Temple people. Adults. He's sitting with them talking.

We stand there a moment, wondering what is going on. Is this really our son? He's totally absorbed in discussion, listening, nodding and occasionally shaking his head. Then, he looks up and sees us on the edge of the crowd. He stands up, seems to say some words of farewell to the men in the group and comes towards us.

I'm as puzzled as I'm angry. What is he doing? Why would he do this to us, to his mother? She's upset, the relief she feels now undoing her calm demeanour. She clings to him, crying.

I draw them away from the crowd, away from the temple to a quieter corner where we can hear each other speak.

'Are you alright, son?' He looks pale, a bit bedraggled. 'Where have you been sleeping? What have you been eating?' He simply nods, shrugs, as though to say, 'Of course, I'm fine'.

We know we need to start our journey home, but we sit awhile and eat some bread and cheese in silence. After a while, he says,

'There's no need to be worried. I thought you'd know where I was.'

We don't know what he means. I glance at his mother. She sits, calm now, quiet, something deep going on inside her. Puzzled, like me. He seems older now, more assured, confident.

I think about these things as we journey back home. There's lots of time to be alone and to think. I remember how it had been in the beginning. How I'd trusted in my dream to keep Miryam as my wife and the sense I'd had that this child was to be special with some role to play in our history.

As I said, we have tried to share our observance of the law and prophets with him. And that is because I trusted the dream, believing it was a holy message. And that is how we will continue with him. If he is meant to be someone, to do something special, it will be revealed.

It is so good to get back home to Nazareth and fall back into our routine.

2.5 Crafting a yoke[49]

Reading

Matthew 6:25-34; 11:25-29; 23:1-12; Luke 12:22-34; Sirach (Ecclesiasticus) 6:24, 24:19-21, 51:23-30, Jeremiah 18:1-13, Isaiah 64:8

---

[49] Instructions informed by several sources, including Building an Ox Yoke – Tillers International www.tillersinternational.org/s/Building-an-Ox-Yoke-TechGuide.pdf

Context

Wisdom as an aspect of God is a strong theme in Jewish theology. It is evident in Hebrew Scriptures, and especially in the 'Wisdom Books', such as Job, Proverbs, the Book of Wisdom, and Ecclesiasticus (or Ben Sir/Sirach). In some writings, Wisdom is personified as 'Sophia'. Early Christian writers identified Jesus with Sophia, the feminine Wisdom of God. There are notable references to Wisdom throughout Matthew's Gospel. The parallels between Matthew 11:28-30 and the Sirach references above are obvious, with the evangelist putting the words of Sophia into the mouth of Jesus – with obvious powerful implications about the community's belief about Jesus.

2.5a 'My yoke is easy'

Some years ago, my husband was renovating his father's former home in Chennai. The place had seen little attention in the twenty years since my father-in-law's death. Bricks, sand and timber were delivered along the suburban street on a flat-trayed cart pulled by a bullock. A wooden yoke rested on the bullock's shoulders. A carpenter came in the mornings. He squatted in the yard, measuring out lengths with string and pencil. He sawed, chiselled and planed the heavy teak by hand, shaping it into beds and tables and stools. If Joseph worked in wood, were these the kind of products that he and Jesus would have made? And did they make wooden yokes to be worn by bullocks?

To make a yoke...

First, one finds wood fit for the task from the local forest. Juniper is strong and works well with shaping. Oak provides a sturdy yoke for heavy work. Pine or sycamore are lighter for simple ploughing.

> anxious to be done
> they go out early past fields –
> red, yellow, blue, white –
> poppies, mustard, wildflowers
> unconcerned about sunset

For the bow, one needs to go deep into the woods to find a young sapling reaching tall beneath the canopy. Only then will it be straight and free from knots which can weaken it.

> the archer
> releases his arrow straight
> towards its mark
> searching a place to rest
> I long for you, O God

> grimy, bone-sore
> and salty with sweat
> they return,
> walking slowly in time
> with talk of things that matter

When the timber's seasoned, the tools are laid out – adze, chisel, mallet, knife, hatchet and auger: time to cut and smooth the yoke piece, chisel out the slots to hold the bow and pegs.

> from lumpen clay
> a deep bowl takes shape
> on the potter's wheel
> earthen and easily broken
> you form me in your hands

The bow that loops beneath the creature's head needs to soak and soften in steam above a fire, bent to form a loop. The craftsman's sinews and muscles arc in tension with the wood. From small pieces come the pegs that will hold the bows in place.

> though she moves slowly
> age-bent and pain-twisted,
> her song is still clear:
> *in your hands I am safe*
> *leaning on you I'm secure*

Now one shapes the yoke to make it curve neatly around the particular beast for whom it's made. The yoke should fit well, neither loose nor tight, with just enough space to fit a hand between the oxen's neck and the wood. Plane and polish it. Smooth it with a shard of pottery, so it will not chafe the working beast.

Finally, one puts the piece aside to let it season slowly: as the green wood dries, the yoke becomes much lighter.

It takes skill and care to make a yoke that is easy to bear.

2.5b Yokes that chafe

Reading

Matthew 11:28-30

There are so many children, women and men bound to unkind yokes...

harnessed
to plough furrows
of devastation,
the children, women, men
in wars of others' making

lonely men
in no-man's land,
offshore detention,
beyond endurance
harnessed to hopelessness

a family
asks for a place
they might call home –
we offer
crude wooden legalism

she counts the days
and measures out her dollars
on welfare
chafed by the harshness
of 'bootstraps philosophy'

government
makes big promises
when we're in need
bureaucratic gobbledegook
breaks our backs

long years ago
they recognised their love
had failed –
still, they wait, bound in chains
pending church annulment

the ox stumbles
beneath the weight
of heavy timber –

> a mindset of law
> overshadows its spirit
>
> heed the teaching
> of Rabbis, Elders, Priests –
> but follow him
> whose yoke fits easily,
> words sized to what we can bear

Something to think about

The word 'God' expresses something of the mystery at the heart of our religious search. It comes from the Sanskrit word, *ghu-to*, meaning 'called one'. 'We do not see his face; we do not hear his voice; yet we sense his presence at the heart of our lives, calling us.' That is, 'God' is the one we call, who in turn calls to us in our depths.[50]

*

'But because you are a forgiving God, gracious (*hannun*) and compassionate (*rahum*), patient and rich in faithful love (*hesed*), you did not abandon them.'[51]

*

'The Lord passed in front of him proclaiming, "The LORD, the LORD, a compassionate and gracious God, slow to anger and abounding in steadfast love and fidelity, who shows mercy to thousands. He forgives iniquity and

---

[50] Michael Fallon msc, *The Four Gospels. An introductory commentary*, Catholic Adult Education Centre, Sydney, 1981, page 4.
[51] Nehemiah 9:17.

transgression and sin, but will by no means forgive the iniquity of the fathers..."'[52]

*

Jesus knew the peasant world well. 'He knew the importance of ploughing a straight line without looking back. He knew the sometimes-unrewarded labour of the sowers. He saw that seeds could only germinate deep in the ground, and the farmer never knew how the seedlings grow. He knew how hard it is to separate the wheat from the seeds... and how patiently one must wait for the fig tree to bear fruit.'[53]

---

[52] Exodus 34:6-7.
[53] Juan Pagola, *Jesus. An historical approximation*, Convivium Press, Miami, 2009 (2015 edition), page 61.

3
Going public

Bedouin donkey, Wadi Qelt, Judean mountains

3.1 Jesus leaves home

Reading

Deuteronomy 24:17-22, Micah 6:8, Proverbs 3

Place

It is several days' walk from Nazareth in the northern region of Galilee towards the desert area on the eastern side of the Jordan.

Context

Around 28CE, when Jesus is about 31-34, something moves him to leave his work, his family and Nazareth. He is unmarried. It is likely that his father Joseph has died. At a time when life expectancy is around 40 years, that is, quite late in his life, he makes a radical decision and severs his ties with his family and village. This is not well-received by his family. Only his mother and his brother James will later join him.

3.1a Leaving home

Most of us leave home at some time. For different reasons: to study, to explore, to take up a career, to break free from dependency, control, sometimes from violence; to find a partner and establish our own home, to make a pilgrimage. Whenever we leave home, we are, in one way or another, seeking our way, the way we are called to.

> you set out
> from Nazareth
> walking
> into uncertainty, already
> a scandal to the village

It is late in life for you to make such a change, leaving the familiar for the unknown, the predictable for the unpredictable, the accepted way of life for one that is less acceptable.

> going away
> from where you're known,
> from what you know
> driven by discontent
> always seeking home

Where does this dissatisfaction in you come from? What unsettles your sense of the way things are? Is it in the grinding lives of those you see in Nazareth? Is there a memory from your childhood of peasant bodies hanging crucified along the roadway by Roman occupiers? Bodies who had names and children in the village?

> from childhood
> you'd heard psalms
> of a steadfast God –
> a covenant with Israel
> and justice for the poor

> searching always
> for silver, rubies, the gold
> of Wisdom
> your words a treasure
> held close within me

Have you heard people tell of different prophets calling for purification around the country? And about one they call 'baptiser' – a man called John – who is preaching baptism and repentance in the south of the country around the river Jordan?

> your brothers say
> your family needs you,
> you're a fool –
> whose voice speaks so
> quietly and insistently?
>
> the risk
> of leaving all behind
> a smaller risk ....
> than to snub
> a Spirit who disturbs

3.1b An unlikely mentor

Reading

Matthew 3:1-6, 11:2-6, 11:7-15, Mark 1:2-6, Luke 3:1-6, John 1:19-28, Isaiah 40:3-5

Place

The desert area east of the Jordan was under the Governor Herod Antipas. While John's Gospel mentions the Baptiser being 'in Bethany across the Jordan', the Baptiser seems to have moved around to spread his teaching, so there is probably no one place where he preached and baptised.

Context

John was a prophet and baptiser who chose to work in the wilderness, away from the temple and its rituals, outside the institution. It was at Jericho that Joshua led the Chosen People into the Promised Land. If, as some scholars suggest, John at some time preached near Jericho, it was a reminder to his contemporaries of Israel's long years wandering through the desert and that the Jewish people – through their corruption – were once again outside the Promised Land.

John the Baptiser features several times in the Gospels. The Gospels portray in John someone who exercised an important role for Jesus. Their close relationship was known to his disciples who let Jesus know when John was beheaded. Jesus had great regard for John, praising him as *the greatest person around*.

From prison, John sent a message to Jesus asking if he were 'the one' ...

An observer's view of John

There he is, a wild man, hair ungroomed, half-dressed in bits of fur he's taken from a camel. Gaunt and bony. He's standing on the bank beside the river, beckoning to the poor devils who are crowding around.

'Repent,' he shouts, his voice hoarse. It is not a gentle voice. Not a welcoming voice. Harsh, rough, grating. He's been at it for hours now. I've been watching at a distance. Not welcoming, but it's impossible not to be moved by him. He's so frenzied, maybe a little crazy after all that time in the back-blocks, but certainly convincing.

And they come. They keep on coming. Crowds. Out here in the bush, streaming away from the towns, from the city. Look at them – hobbling along on sticks, old women, beggars. Women of the night. Screaming lunatics. Probably lepers too if I checked. Sinners all of them.

He shouts again, 'Repent, change your hearts, turn around your lives,[54] prepare for the Lord's coming.'

And they love it. All these poor god-forsakens, here in the wilderness with this madman, wanting more. They're looking for something they're not finding in the temple. Looking for repentance. Looking for the Lord. They call out: 'What should I do to repent?' There were soldiers here before and they asked. Even a tax collector. Everyone is asking, wanting his direction. And what he tells them is about being fair, not cheating people, about sharing food and clothing. It's a while since I've heard that sort of talk from a teacher. If you call this wild man a teacher.

See them line up. He's leading them now into the water and they're confessing they are sinners. What right has he got to ask them to confess to him? He pushes them down, right down into the water until they come up spluttering. And laughing too. They seem happy about it.

---

[54] The Greek word used, *metanoia*, literally translates as something more than 'repentance' and involves 'turning around the way you think', having a 'complete change of heart', changing the lens through which you view life.

Earlier on when some teachers and priests approached him, he turned on them, and called them snakes. He talked of taking axes to trees that don't bear fruit and fire – it was clear he meant them. As I said, not a gentle man.

It will not end well for this man. Some teachers and priests will not like that. I know, because I am one of them.

> in the desert
> an upstart prophet
> recognises
> longing for redemption
> within those on life's-edge

3.1c Seeking Wisdom

Reading

Isaiah 40:3-5, Proverbs 1, Proverbs 2, Psalm 119, Luke 7:24-30, John 3:22-30

Seeking wisdom through John

After leaving Nazareth, Jesus meets up with John and spends time with him in the wilderness. Jesus sees how the anti-institutional John attracts the poor and marginalised. They are excluded from religious practice in the temple, but John welcomes them. He makes a space for them, speaks to them, offers them a future of better relationship with God.

> he burdens
> no blame on sinners
> who open their hearts –
> we all need to go
> where we find food

Jesus is an observant Jew from a deeply religious Jewish family. He has been immersed in the Torah and practices of Judaism from his childhood. It has shaped a worldview especially attentive to the Roman oppression of his people, hypocrisy in religious observance especially amongst leaders, the suffering of the destitute, sick and outcasts.

> in our land
> the poor sleep homeless
> families beg refuge
> old people are neglected
> who shall be called blameless?

> should I follow
> this instinct, take
> up this position?
> is this my path
> to fulfilment, my call?

> at night
> I toss and turn
> worrying
> will I ever learn
> to become good

> my heart is set
> on seeking Wisdom
> sleepless at night
> I search the stars to map
> my path towards righteousness

John's fiery rough rhetoric puts God in centre-place: John wants things straightened out between God and his people. He wants everyone to see God's saving action. He expects that action to be imminent. His words echo those of the prophet Isaiah underscoring his own prophetic role to make straight the way of the Lord.

> a quiver
> of spring leaves
> shifts the air
> something monumental
> is happening here

Jesus becomes a follower of John, accepting him as a prophet and joins him in preaching a baptism of repentance. In this decision, he chooses the way of the prophet, working independently of the religious institution, while remaining a faithful practising Jew. Meanwhile, John has been making a name and enemies for himself, castigating religion that controls, excludes and does not liberate.

Jesus then goes one step further.

3.2 Immersion in his mission

Reading

Mark 1:9-11, Matthew 3:13-17, Luke 3:21-23a, John 1:24-34

Place

The Jordan is fed from waters from Mt Hermon, on the border between Syria and Lebanon, flowing down through the Sea of Galilee and onward down to the Dead Sea, 250 kilometres in all. South of Galilee, it flows between Golan Heights and Jordan to the east, and the West Bank and Israel to the west.

Context

Sometime after meeting John, Jesus makes his decision: he chooses baptism. His baptism is public. He takes a stand. Declares his position.

The Greek word 'baptism' *has meanings that are precise and rich. Primarily, it means to be overwhelmed – to be totally submerged in the truth of something, to be swept off one's feet by something or by someone.*[55]

3.2a Jordan water 2012

At Banias, a group of us climbs over limestone rocks to the looming cave where once people worshipped the god Pan. It is a hot day, early in Spring. The air is fragrant with the sweet scent of figs and bees flurry amongst the leaves. The fruit is still unripe, the green shade heavy with sweetness.

---

[55] Frank Anderson, page 15.

From deep springs, it is here that the Jordan River begins its journey through history. The water splashes down over rocks and rushes through a narrow cutting. The river is clear, revealing brown fish above the round black pebbles on the stream's bed.

We rest beside its noisy tumbling clarity.

> freed from rocks,
> the stream rushes
> in a torrent –
> sometimes in my life
> the way forward is so clear[56]

South of the lake, at a place called Yardenit, the Jordan broadens into a green deep flow. Some claim it is the site of 'Bethany beyond Jordan' which John's Gospel describes as the place of Jesus' baptism. The waters are cool and inviting as they continue south in a wide sweep between overhanging eucalyptus and squat palms.

There is a café and the inevitable tourist shop. A platform has been built with a ramp leading down into the waters. A group of men and women from the Philippines, dressed in white, line up along the ramp leading down into the river. They move forward and immerse themselves. There are photographs taken. There are prayers and laughter. I sense the significance, trying to imagine the moment of immersion.

> I step
> into slow-moving
> waters
> cold shocks
> my limbs and skin

---

[56] A previous version of the first paragraph and opening lines were published in *Elemental Moods*, a chap book written in collaboration with Amelia Fielden, Keitha Keyes, Marilyn Humbert and Jan Foster.

the current
drags me with its flow
knows my body
through and through
cooling, cleansing

I sink down
lose my footing
go under
overwhelmed
till I surrender

to the power
of death, of life,
I rise back up
and grasp the light
as though for the first time

When Jesus asks John to baptise him, something extraordinary happens to him: *an insight as sharp as the brightest light, an assurance as gentle as air moving with a dove's wings.*[57] He is loved, he is the beloved son, of God and God is his father.

3.3 Desert and isolation

Reading

Exodus, namely 13-14, 34, 40, Deuteronomy 26:4-10, Jeremiah 31, Psalm 23, Matthew 4: 1-11, Mark 1:12-13, Luke 4:1-13

---

[57] I am unsure if these are my words or taken from my readings. If the latter, I have been unable to track down their source and apologise to the author.

Place

The desert is a powerful element in the story of the Jewish people. For someone like Jesus, nurtured in a religious home, with some education in the local synagogue and possibly literate in biblical Hebrew, the desert would hold multi-layered associations.

Central to Jewish faith is the memory of their ancestors' long passage from slavery in Egypt to the Promised Land. This was a time of desert wandering, during which they were mindful of the presence of God always with them, guiding them by day as cloud and by night as fire; a time in which God entered again into covenant with them.

The desert is also a hiding place for bandits, a place of banishment, wilderness and isolation. The prophet Hosea refers to the desert also as a place of conversion and fresh starts. And, about 600 years before the time of Jesus, the prophet Jeremiah promised the Jewish people, who were miserable and lamenting in exile in Babylon, that their God would rescue them; that they would find favour in the wilderness, or as the Jerusalem Bible reads, 'pardon in the desert', and they would find rest.

Context

After his baptism, the synoptic Gospels report, Jesus went off by himself into the desert. Wherever Jesus spent his days following his baptism, he was in a deserted and wild place. He has stepped forward for John's baptism. What happens in the desert of the following solitary nights and days? How is Jesus' understanding of himself in relation to God shifting? What happens to etch conviction into the sands of his searching?

3.3a Wadi Qelt 2012

With first light, the desert hills below me are smudged with morning haze. It is crisp, rather than cold, and at first all I hear is the crunch of limestone shale beneath the leather of my sandals. The grass that is here is sparse. Growing in stumpy clumps, it is as still as the rocks. Then, I hear something distant.

> lifted by currents
> the call of a bird[58]
> I lift my eyes
> and open my heart
> to hear the voice of God

With dawn, colours shift across the hills of Moab, indigo to many shades of purple. The valleys are deep in shadow still hiding the tints of green that hint at the proximity of water. Some Bedouins approach, tempting us with their meagre jewellery and handicrafts. Their homes are in the distance, a temporary camp of lean-tos and leftovers. A bedraggled donkey grazes the threadbare shale. And sheep, too, in a far-off gully.

> my nights
> are restless with dreams
> of bringing change –
> I wake in early light
> beside quiet waters

---
[58] Previously in *Elemental Moods*

Here, I can understand in a fresh way the psalm we all know well. It is a place where the rolling sameness of bare hills can easily disorientate a walker: *he guides me along the right paths*. Time in this desert, days and nights alone here, thrusts a person into a place where demons from within and danger from without become constants: *I walk through the darkest valley*. Shelter from the heat of the day, a broth of weeds in evening, shiver through the night: *he makes me lie down in green pastures*. Water, shade and nightfall become the focus of each day.

3.3b In the desert

*I will lead you
into the wilderness,
speak fondly to you
of my everlasting love
my unfailing kindness*

camouflaged
in patterns of sand
a viper
hisses at me
all my fears

a fierce wind whirls
and leaves nothingness –
on each side
red dunes
stretch trackless

all is silent
in this solitude
scratching
the desiccation
of my spirit

I crawl
into thin shade –
an acacia tree
gives shelter
to my emptiness

something moves,
a lizard edges into view,
barely panting
I raise my head
look around me:

shrubby thyme
white-blossoming broom
red anemones
buttercups, wild mustard
the desert teems with life

I breathe out,
slowly, let go my fear
into the silence
let go the need to know,
the need to have control

>   red desert dust   *I will lead you*
>   invades every crevice –   *into the wilderness,*
>   vast deserts   *speak fondly to you*
>   that we inhabit   *of my everlasting love*
>   inhabit us[59]   *my unfailing kindness*

3.3c Grace in the wilderness

All your life, you've been immersed in the teachings and promises. You are a man, at the peak of life, working as a designer, builder, constructing things – a positive role, a useful role for the community.

Do you need to be alone, to go away from all the daily details that distract you from unravelling your purpose, from unveiling it, seeing – at least, a direction?

Do you set out seeking space and solitude? Are you led to reach down into the essence of your being where you'd always found the Wisdom of your God?

Do you set off into the desert, out into the wilderness to go within? I imagine you travelled light. Little food, no clear route planned, journeying rather than journeying to.

Do you sense it as a passage from the familiar to the strange? The domestic to the wilds, led not by a fiery angel or a cloud, but by a still quiet voice within?

And as you walk, day after day, whom do you meet? Travelling tribesmen with whom you share a meal and pass some time? Do you notice small birds in the saltbush, the blues of desert flowers?

Do you walk and rest, eat a little bread, find rhythm in your days? Sit awhile to watch the sun set behind darkening hills, mark your way by stars, and sleep?

---

[59] The 'red desert dust...' is adapted from Matthew del Nevo page 103.

Do you let the questions in your heart rise and fall from morning to evening, patient to wait for the answers to take shape?

Then, after some days, perhaps a storm of delirium and doubt? Do you wander, head down in search of shelter, to find a cave until it passes? Hungry, parched, tempted. Singing psalms into the stars, finding food, resting, remembering the great story of your people loved by God.

Is that how it was?

3.3d Temptations in our desert times

>round and golden
>baked by the sun
>if only those stones
>were bread to end my torment
>of hunger ...for you, my God
>
>a wonder drug –
>some slick spectacular –
>would make people take notice
>of me – the word of God
>grows true but slowly
>
>there are people willing
>to follow me fighting
>might against might –
>my God champions the blind,
>poor, and mothers in labour

Jesus comes back from his desert preaching the reign of God: here, now. A reign of mercy and compassion.

3.4 Beginning his ministry

Reading

Matthew 4:12-22, Mark 1:14-20, Luke 5:1-11, John 1:35-42, Luke 4:14-15, Matthew 14:1-5

Place

When John is imprisoned Jesus returns to Galilee. He does not go home to Nazareth but to Capernaum which, is on the shores of the Sea of Galilee, about 32 kilometres – or a good day's walk – from Nazareth. Peter and Andrew, from Bethsaida, live in Capernaum. Andrew has been a disciple of John the Baptiser and so is probably known to Jesus. Capernaum is also a bit out of the way of Herod Antipas who has had John jailed.

Much of the ancient township has been uncovered by archaeologists to reveal dry-stone walls and narrow ways between the dwellings. One of these is regarded as the home of Peter.

Context

Here Jesus continues the preaching he has started when with John. Initially, he simply takes on John's teaching: *Repent*

for the kingdom of God is near. Gradually, like any good teacher, he modifies his teaching as he comes into his own authority. Not just repent, but *the time is fulfilled, and the kingdom of God has come near.*

He starts to gather people around him. He distinguishes himself from John and his disciples, who fast, by feasting – with the poor and outcast, with the wealthy and with Pharisees.

The first followers he invites are those he already knows, two sets of brothers, Peter and Andrew, James and John. Living as they do on the shores of the Sea, they are all fishermen. Andrew and Simon have a friend Philip who has also followed John.

This reflection weaves together strands from the Synoptics and John's Gospel.

3.4a Come and See... Andrew's story

Simon and I have been spending some time with John for a while now; when we hear he is nearby, we stop work and go to listen to him. These are troubled times and somehow his call to turn around our hearts touches me. How do I live a good life as taught by the Law and Prophets?

So, we were with John one day and this man walked by. John pointed him out to us: he looked like just another fellow, no different from the rest of us. But because of what John, said, we kept our eyes on him, this Jesus. One day, we were trailing along behind him trying to see why John had singled him out, and he stopped. He turned, and laughing at our awkwardness, asked 'What do you want? What are you looking for?'

>   feeling foolish
>   caught out like a thief
>   I cannot
>   find words enough
>   for what I look for

'Where are you staying?' we ask him. Meaning, we haven't seen you around John before. And, quite relaxed, he shrugs with a smile, 'Come and see.'

>   he invites us
>   to see for ourselves
>   who he is
>   within the intimacy
>   of his own space

So, we went with him and spent the rest of the day with him.

This man follows John like us, but he breathes something different – I want to call it Wisdom. He sees things differently from the rest of us. He shares our meals. He lives like us. Yet when he speaks, it's as if he sees things I do not see and puts together, all the patchwork of our lives into one seamless cloak. Who else would tell us God is like a child?

Where does it come from? This crystal conviction that seems to be growing stronger even as we speak – that God Almighty, deliverer of Moses and the Israelites, who brought us back from captivity and exile is – so close, so fine, so compassionate?

>   in dust and drought
>   when you can hardly breathe
>   for hopelessness
>   God is in the breeze,
>   a sprinkle of cool water

When we left, we bubbled with excitement and
confusion. Had we just spent the afternoon with someone
who would become the promised one, the Messiah? Even if
he came from Nazareth?

3.4b The call of Simon and his brother

... How did it happen?
Might it have gone something like this
or something completely other?
You hear that Antipas has imprisoned John –

so you head towards the lake and there
within the simple things – the breeze,
the squelch of gravel, lap of wavelets taking breath
and sighing– you hear larks and wonder

what this means now? Do you realise
something that you've known one way or other
since you were a child above the Jezreel Plains?
A quiver in the essence of yourself?

Is that where you find them, or they find you,
the fishermen, Simon and his brother?
Do you sit and watch the poem of their fishing
as they cast their nets and heave to draw them in,

the shrug of disappointment, the separation of
small from big? The leader, Simon, urging on his team
to try again, grumbling at their slowness
and their lack of trust.

Did you start chatting then, talking of the catch,
the wind, the depths, until he asks you what you do –

a muscle-hardened worker by the shore, with time to spend?
And did you say, 'I'm looking for some men,

some men like you, to help me in my father's business,'?
Did Simon scratch his head and ask, 'Work?
What work? He has a boat? 'Round here?'
'No, not like that, well, not exactly,' you might have said.

Simon shakes his head, 'You're talking riddles, Mate,
but come and have a drink. We're going home.'
And in the evening, over food and wine, do you tell him
that you like his courage and persistence, a man who leads,

a chap who's seen a bit of life? 'You know we've met before,
with John.' Do you ask him if he's heard what's happened,
and how he's now in jail? Simon shaking sunburned head,
while his womenfolk click their tongues aghast.

'Why do they fear him?' Simon asks. 'He was calling
for repentance, change, about more than outwardly
observance.' And did you say, 'The time for change has come;
it's what my father wants of me. I need you to help me'?

Volunteers, always hard to get in any enterprise,
especially a new untested one; a scheme that's sure to prove
unpopular, at best uncertain: was it your conviction
that swayed them to think of following you?

And did Simon say, as darkness comes and the smell of
fire-smoke is in the air, 'Look, I guess I don't quite get
what this is you're asking for, but I've heard you've
done good things. Come back tomorrow and we'll talk some more.'

And do you leave him then, his family and their home
and wander back towards the lake and to the cave
you've been using for your sleep to spend the night?

3.5 Who is this man?

Reading

Luke 4:31-44, 5:16, 6:12, 9:18, 28, 11:1, Mark 1:32-39, Matthew 8:16-17

Place

Kefar Nahum, the village of Nahum

This episode begins in Capernaum beside the Sea of Galilee. The Sea is beautiful, peaceful. There are places near Capernaum where the terrain slopes up from the water, places where one can walk and sit quietly in reflection. There are hills that can be climbed to offer seclusion and a long view over the calming view of the Sea. In the early morning there is a freshness in the air; the soft cries of small black birds; shade under an overhanging ledge. The Sea changes colour with the sun and heat and clouds and wind. Sometimes, it shines almost emerald.

The partially restored synagogue whose limestone ruins stands there now was built around the 4th or 5th century CE on the site of an earlier synagogue which dates from first century CE, the time of Jesus. In Luke 7:1-10, we read of a Roman centurion who had built a synagogue in Capernaum because of his regard for the people. The Sea is visible through the doors of the synagogue.

Context

Jesus is beginning to get busy. He is developing a reputation as a preacher and a healer – driving out demons from a man in the synagogue in Capernaum and healing many people at Simon's house, including Peter's own mother-in-law. As an observant Jew immersed in the Law of Moses, all he did was referenced to the will of God: what did God want of him? Presumably he observed the daily routine of prayers at set times and blessings over food. Prayer – connecting with God, understanding God's will for him – was like breathing. His worldview was religious.

Luke shows Jesus interrupting his missionary activities regularly to withdraw and pray. This is often at night and on a mountain top: a place where one can feel removed from the trivia of daily life and somehow closer to God; mountain tops were also traditional locations in the history of Israel where the presence of God was specially experienced. The outstanding instance of Jesus spending the night in prayer is the night of anguish on the Mount of Olives just before his arrest. The event known as the Transfiguration seems to have occurred during another such night of prayer.

3.5a Breathing prayer

People have heard about him. They come to him, in the evening, at sundown: the sick, the mentally ill, crippled, those who were not welcome to roam the streets in daylight. The people of the shadows – whom society would prefer to forget. In Mark's account, 'the whole city was gathered around the door'. A press of people. People in need. We can try to imagine the surge – the jostle and cacophony of the desperately hopeful, the odours of animals, dust, labourers and the ill.

Jesus responded to them. He did not send them away. He met them, felt their suffering, touched them, and allowed their humanity to touch him. Some were cured.

Jesus should have been tired. Yet, in Mark's account, Jesus is something of a light sleeper. He rises while it is still dark to go alone to a quiet place to pray. Is it that the distress and poverty he sees weighs upon him? Does the fact that his interventions leave some people cured disturb him? Is his sleep being overtaken by the electric energy of his mission taking clearer shape? He does not slip away alone just so that he can think things through: he goes to pray. He goes to immerse himself in God.

When they wake and find him missing, Simon and his companions – presumably Andrew his brother, and James and John – look for him. There is a sense that, even early in the morning, people have come to Simon's house to find Jesus, this man from Nazareth who is healing and teaching. Perhaps, they have waited overnight to see him in the early hours before they slink away out of sight.

> He rises early in the morning
> seeking to be alone to pray
> carrying with him the cries
> reaching him from other towns.
>
> His instinct seems to be
> to seek his God within
> his deepest self as one.
> Is it here, conviction
> is forged in solitude? –

not more of the same
not just carrying on
because the crowd is there,
the difference between dizziness
and the Father's business.

Was he put off by the crowds?
Did all the publicity strike
a chord of uncertainty?
*Is this what I'm about? Why
I've abandoned family, home and
normal expectations?* How reply
to his brothers' criticisms,
and the questioning
expression of his mother?

He returns to these new friends –
they're all pumped up with crowds
of people at the house – but he
is clear. *Let's go
somewhere else...*
to teach in other villages nearby:
That's why I've come.

Something to think about

Matthew del Nevo writes of people who spend time in deserts. To dwell and survive in the desert, he writes, is to become lost in silence and listening. 'To know this silence and listening is to understand the desert as the original place of theology. To abide in this silence and listening is to *pray truly*...

'The spiritual tradition of the *Shekinah*, the divine presence, which was with the Israelites in the wilderness, means that the promised land, or the ideal city, is never literally *beyond*, but projects what is already *present: God with us*. The *Shekinah* is the *absence* of any place of true abode beyond itself. The language of God's presence is essentially a desert language, it is dispossessive. Dispossessive language is... a language that learns to let go of itself and listen. I think that the desert is the only environment in which this language can be understood.'[60]

*

In his essay on silence, poet David Whyte writes, 'Silence is frightening, an intimation of the end, the graveyard of fixed identities. Real silence puts any present understanding to shame; orphans us from certainty; leads us beyond the well-known and accepted reality and confronts us with the unknown and previously unacceptable conversation about to break in upon our lives... In silence, essence speaks to us of essence itself...'[61]

---

[60] Matthew del Nevo, 'Desert Literature, Desert Language,' in Michael Griffith, Ross Keating (eds). *Religion, Literature and the Arts Project: Conference Proceedings of the Australian International Conference 1994.* Sydney: Australian Catholic University, 1994. https://openjournals.library.sydney.edu.au/index.php/SSR/issue/view/849/ pages 102-108.

[61] Whyte, D. 'Silence', in *Consolations: The solace, nourishment and underlying meaning of everyday words.* Langley WA, Many Rivers Press, 2015.

4
Yeshua: Teacher

Early morning by the Sea of Galilee, near Tabgha, Galilee

4.1 Where he worked

Reading

Luke 9:1-12, Mark 6:14-18

Place

During the short period of his public life, Jesus taught, healed and preached in a small area. Scholars refer to it as his teaching triangle from Chorazin north of the Sea of Galilee, to Bethsaida, some 9-10 kilometres to the south east, across to Tiberias, Capernaum and Tabgha in the south west. The Sea, also known as the Lake of Tiberias, itself is about 53 kilometres around, 21 kilometres from north to south, about 12 kilometres from west to east. The name has changed over time; Luke calls it the Lake of Gennesaret.

The Sea is large enough for storms to blow up and at 43 metres is deep enough to be dangerous. In recent years, the signs of climate change are evident with the area of water noticeably shrinking in some parts.

The stories of feeding large numbers of people are believed to have taken place on the Sea somewhere near Tabgha, about half an hour's walk from Capernaum.

Context

Word about Jesus is spreading and reaches Herod Antipas. He is a powerful and dangerous enemy. Jesus moves his area of work away from Herod Antipas who had already been so threatened by the popular responses to John the Baptiser's preaching.

4.1a Walking

I discovered the richness of walking later in life. I walk to exercise responsibility for my health – investing in my future. I've learned that walking is as much about the mind and spirit as it is about stretching one's limbs and lungs. I am indebted to friends and my children who have accompanied my walking – in every sense of accompaniment.

Eventually, I enjoyed the deep richness of walking in pilgrimage on the Camino in Spain. I learned while walking in Spain to find my own path, and to live at my own pace, not that of others; to travel according to my calling; that it is prudent to travel light; yet, if travelling unencumbered takes courage, it also brings its own freedom; that every walk is a pilgrimage, even if it is to collect the mail from Toongabbie post office. Every walk is a journey towards home.

> we follow one path
> on our different journeys
> constantly shifting
> the baggage we carry
> in search of the essential
>
> quiet comes
> on a slower pace,
> a gentler path
> the place I'm seeking
> opens up to me[62]

Jesus did a lot of walking. So many hours and days for talking with companions and those along the way; opportunities for silence, feeling the beauty, harshness and rhythms of nature, observing people or watching them work,

---

[62] Two tanka previously published in 'Camino: A Tanka Diary', *Haibun Today*, Volume 10, Number 2, June 2016.

listening to them as he walked along or reflecting, praying with his whole body, maybe walking to the rhythm of the psalms.

4.1b Sea of Galilee

The Sea's colours are hazy and pale in the hot early summer morning, pale grey, almost white. The wind chops the soft blue and tosses white caps to the sky. Soft feathery-branched casuarina-like trees, a fresh pale green at this time of year, stand watch at the edge which is rocky with dark basalt. The Sea sighs against the stones.

>   a fishing boat
> rides the sea in rhythm
>   with the current
>   men throw a net
> and haul in their catch

It is a restful place, even with tourist-pilgrims. Early in the morning and in the evenings, it is still and quiet. Apart from the gentle lapping, the only sounds are those of birds – small birds, that rise and swoop above fish that sometimes jump up out of the water and plop back in; larger white birds, higher, further from the shore, who swoop down and skim the surface.

Nearby, there are doves, starlings, sparrows, larks, warblers.

Hills slope up from the water. A pleasing place to sit, to relax, to come from the village chores and watch the soft blue of the waters fade into the soft sky. Cypress, pine and more recent eucalyptus scattered across the hillside. In the distance, on the other side of the Sea, are the hazy beige blue hills of Golan.

I sit and ponder the immediacy of the place where Jesus walked, sailed, fished and bathed.

> on the shore below
> murmuring pilgrims
> crunch over stones –
> the Sea shimmers
> with stories

4.1c Bethsaida

I was strongly moved when I visited the place that some archaeologists identify as Bethsaida. The site is now about two kilometres from the present shore of the Sea. Climate change continues to raise the temperature of the waters of the Sea, resulting in significant impacts on the ecosystem of the Sea. There are fears that continued temperature increases will render its waters unusable. This has been compounded by intensive use of the waters for irrigation, resulting in low water levels around the shoreline.

Two upright basalt markers (steles) at the entrance to the town are on the site of a large gatehouse, suggesting Bethsaida's significance possibly 1000 years before New Testament times. Excavations from Hellenistic and early Roman times have identified a two-storey 'winemaker's house' and a single-story 'fisherman's house'.

Our guide – a reputable scholar – claims the paving is authentically 1st century CE. I am walking where Jesus once walked. My imagination is totally ill-formed about the realities of the time, but nonetheless, that does not stop me from conjuring up lives being lived there.

> women grind
> grain with basalt mortars
> the air thick
> with the morning's catch –
> your neighbours and kin
>
> walking
> where you trod
> in your space
> breathing in a sense
> of real presence

4.2 His teaching: a kingdom of God

Place

Despite it being understood as unlikely for a village so small to have its own synagogue, tradition claims a site for a synagogue in ancient Nazareth. Some scholars agree there are signs of a synagogue and a ritual bath from this time. Alternate views suggest that the synagogue prayers might have been conducted outdoors or in a courtyard; or there may have been a synagogue in the larger village of Japhia, a kilometre and a half away.

Context

As Jesus continues his work, he wins over some people and unsettles others. While he observes the Law and religious practices, there are some elements that he challenges.

The *kingdom* or *reign of God* becomes the core of Jesus' teaching. The term *reign of God* (or the *kingdom of Heaven*) is used 120 times in the Gospels of Matthew, Mark and Luke. In Luke's account of Jesus preaching in the synagogue at Nazareth, there is a clear alignment between Jesus and the Messiah prefigured in the reading from Isaiah. This Gospel traces Jesus' baptism by John, his trials in the desert, being found by the vulnerable and needy and his time spent in prayer. Luke then goes on to portray Jesus as a teacher who begins to speak out and speak up with determination, urgency and without inhibition.

4.2a Signalling the kingdom in Nazareth

Reading

Luke 4:14-30, Mark 6:1-6, Matthew 13:54-58, Psalm 146, Isaiah 61:1-3, Isaiah 42:1-7

Jesus comes to his hometown, Nazareth.

> her son has come home
> for a while, his mum says,
> baking extra bread
> – nosy neighbours a-chatter
> with what they've heard he's done
>
> *did you know*
> *women ask their menfolk*
> *he's a healer,*
> *a teacher? One of us!*
> words slippery with meaning

In the synagogue on the Sabbath, he chooses a reading from Isaiah, startling (and alienating) his neighbours with the clarity of his words.

> *I have*
> *good news for you all:*
> *our God is here,*
> *near... especially*
> *to those who hurt*

Did he say to them: 'You know who I mean? That woman from the bazaar, whom you're quick to condemn, and some of you men are just as ready to visit at night? Exploiting her need to support her children? And Asher's son, the one with the crippled foot? Or those ragamuffin children with pus-filled eyes and scabby legs who steal your figs and bread because they're hungry? The beggars at the entrance to the village in their grubby rags whom you carefully avoid? The distressed old man Chaim who screams profanities as we walk by? Or that dark-skinned family who've arrived here in our village and don't seem quite like you?'

And did he say: 'This is what I yearn for? From my very bowels, I long for the blind to see the colours of the wildflowers and the faces of their brothers and sisters and to see in them the wonder of God; for those we pretend do not exist in our society, those who are despised, criticised and ostracised: I would love to see them sit together in friendship at a table and enjoy the feast of God's compassion; for the broken-hearted: if only they could know the steadfast love of God. And for those in any kind of oppression and prison: let them be freed with unconditional pardons, like the endless mercy of our God. The Most High has sent me to proclaim this news. The Lord has sent me to proclaim this freedom, to comfort the wretched and depressed and to announce the coming of God's reign.'

> this Joseph's son –
> who's he to decide
> good news?
> why would we fall for claims
> that he's the Chosen One?

And the people who were permitted to enter the synagogue begin to grumble. They cry out against him, fingers in their ears to block out news of happiness for the poor and powerless. And turn him away.

4.3 So, what is this kingdom?

Reading

Matthew 5:1-12, Luke 6:17-26, Psalm 37, Psalm 126, Proverbs 8:32, 12:20, Isaiah 51:1-16, 1 Corinthians 1:26-31

Place

In many ways, it doesn't matter where exactly Jesus taught. We know he walked the roads and lakeside in Galilee. The hills near Capernaum make a natural amphitheatre. Where better to speak to large groups of people than by the Sea?

What we know today as the Mount of Beatitudes is a beautiful place. The chapel that has been built there memorialises the *Beatitudes* carefully.

Context

The discourses recalled in Matthew's 'Sermon on the Mount' and Luke's 'Sermon on the Plain' are composites brought together by the evangelists – a kind of compendium that reflects the early Christian community's understanding of their remembered experience of Jesus and of the sorts of things he taught

The Beatitudes are seen as typical of the way Jesus taught, drawing on a model he probably knew from the Wisdom teachings in the Hebrew scriptures.

When will the kingdom come?

4.3a A Big Day Out

By the Sea as crowds of tourist pilgrims gather at what is memorialised (accurately or not) as the Mount of Beatitudes, there is something of a festival air – enthusiastic people, like us, seeking to understand Jesus better. Festive and reflective.

So, too, 2000 years ago, men and women hear Jesus is in the area and follow the crowd along the Sea. Word has been spreading about him. They leave behind their normal routines to seek him out. A motley gathering – the curious, the sceptical, the wistfully hopeful, those persuaded to come along, those seeking diversion – not unlike us today. They've been told about the sort of things he's been saying, want to hear for themselves. There's a picnic atmosphere, anticipation of hearing something to lift their spirits. Not the 'in' crowd, these people massing by the water, not those with access to influence and preference, but the others... all of them.

and he teaches:
happiness for the gentle,
the poor, the grieving,
the foolish who show mercy –
so many contradictions

4.3b If I had been there

If I had been there then, among the ill, the tormented, the unemployed, homeless and the rest of them on one of those days when he taught this way, how might I have felt to hear him say:

You can be happy if you're poor because you that's a sign you belong in God's kingdom.
      Happy? In my filthy rags and destitution?

You're fortunate, you know, even though you're hungry now and your belly growls, for you'll have all you need in the kingdom that is coming.
> Will God give me bread now? And tomorrow?

And those of you who are sad, who are in mourning for those you've lost, believe me, you'll be laughing when God's reign is here. You don't feel it now, I know, but your time will come.
> If you only knew the heavy cloak of sadness that presses on my back and drags behind me in the dust.
> Yet, as you speak, I feel that maybe, maybe, you do know my sadness.

Look, you might feel you're looked down on now. That you're of no account, that you're on the outer, especially because you listen to me. But, when God comes in his kingdom, you'll be dancing for joy. You'll be rewarded then.
> Do I dare to believe you?
> That you're speaking to me?
> For me?

If you're looking for happiness, this is where you'll find it.
> This is too good. This is unbelievable.
> If it is as you say, I should be the happiest person on earth.

4.3c And today, what do I say?

And what do I say, today, if I try to hear him?
 You can be happy if you're poor because you belong in God's kingdom.

Our poor are multiplying. They are still on the edges – as you said they would be. We find them washed up on the shore of Lampedusa, sleeping in doorways on Sydney's footpaths, playing out their hopes on pokies in the Leagues Club, in the riverbed near Alice Springs, sleeping through winter in a car at Blacktown, working three part-jobs to nearly make one living ...

>	my nothingness
>	falls through open fingers
>	hanging on
>	by a flimsy thread
>	to words of mystery

You're fortunate, you know, even though you're hungry now and your belly growls, for you'll have all you need in the kingdom that is coming.

>	our earth burns
>	men, women, children burn
>	power is aflame
>	any small sign of your reign
>	would quicken me

And those of you who are sad, who are in mourning for those you've lost, for all you've lost, believe me, you'll be laughing when God's reign is here. You don't feel it now, I know, but your time will come.

Grief steals up on me in the night, bundles me in a rug that leaves me breathless,
throws me into an ocean current dragging me out to deep dark waters.

You've been chiselled away from me leaving behind desolation.

After All This Time

My heart has become a shop for emptiness[63]

I weep for children damaged and abused, for each hope taken,
for relationships uncherished, un-nurtured, wasted.

I embrace this sadness, own the disappointments in myself,
and confess that I am mourning.

I find peace in accepting my ineffectiveness, my emptied heart
that sees what can only be seen through eyes that have cried.[64]

Look, you might feel you're looked down on now. That you're of no account, that you're on the outer, especially because you listen to me. But, when God comes in his kingdom, you'll be dancing for joy. You'll be rewarded then.

whistle-blowers,
prophets, upright, outspoken:
rejections
are the KPIs
of discipleship

If you're looking for happiness, this is where you'll find it.

be glad
if you're not an A-lister,
if your friend is pain...
you are alive to your self
and the hunger in life

This is your message: *God loves the poor...* What kind of topsy-turvey kingdom is this?

---

[63] The phrase, 'shop for emptiness,' is from the Sufi mystic Rumi.
[64] Attributed to Oscar Romero.

4.4 Within and among us

Reading

The kingdom is here among you: Matthew 11:2-19, Luke 7:18-28, Luke 17:20-21, Mark 1:15, Luke 10:23-24, Isaiah 52:7.
Jesus and exorcisms: Matthew 12:25-32, Luke 11:20, Mark 3:24-27.
Feasting, not fasting: Mark 2:13-19, Luke 5:27-39, Matthew 9:9-17, Luke 7:31-35, Matthew 11:16-20.
Feedings as feasts of the kingdom: Mark 6:30-38, Matthew 14:13-21, Luke 9:10-17, John 6:1-13.

Context

John is in prison and he sends some of his followers to Jesus, asking him if he is the Messiah. Jesus replies in a way that a Jewish prophet would understand very clearly: as the prophet Isaiah had proclaimed, blind receive sight, cripples walk, deaf hear, the poor hear good news.

Jesus has taken up John's mission but shifts it into something different. He goes further than John and begins to speak of the kingdom of God as not just approaching but declares that the kingdom is here, now.

4.4a Can you recognise the kingdom?

The kingdom is both here now and still to be realised. It is in tension between already present and not-yet fulfilled. It is among you.

>   with a potter's skill
>   you re-shape the damaged bowl
>   filling it
>   with joy for crushed hearts
>   ... good news indeed

>   to the broken
>   you offer wholeness,
>   the dejected
>   you enfold in gladness...
>   this is good news indeed

>   can't you see
>   God's power,
>   here and now
>   in each of us,
>   working among us?

>   in this kingdom
>   each one's birthright is mercy
>   the language is joy
>   the currency is kindness...
>   the ruler is called *father*

Exorcisms are not uncommon. There are magicians who make their living by offering their wares and powers to cure those with mental illnesses and affliction.

>   others use charms,
>   spells and incantations,
>   incense and hair –
>   you simply command
>   evil spirits depart

You offend Pharisees and scribes when you eat with tax collectors and those they call sinners – the unclean. John the Baptiser's disciples are also confused because you do not fast.

> in Levi's house
> among undesirables
> you eat and drink
> happy to be with them
> happy to share your news
>
> food and wine
> and joyful fellowship
> the kingdom
> is a wedding feast
> a festive paradigm

The Gospels give reports of different times when large numbers of people are fed from meagre supplies: in each account, as the thousands of people sit on the ground listening to Jesus, their hungers are satisfied – and still there is excess, over and beyond the needs of anyone present.

> from five small fish
> and a few loaves of bread
> so many are filled
> leaving baskets to share
> in a realm of abundance

Food shared with joy strengthens our sense of connection – interconnection – at the same time as it celebrates it. A meal of true fellowship, conversation and laughter nourishes us long after we have left the table.

In the words of theologian Edward Schillebeeckx, Jesus' dealings with people liberate them and make them glad.'[65]

---

[65] Quoted in Edwards, page 47.

4.4b Who is missing?

Reading

Parable of the lost sheep: Luke 15:1-7, Matthew 18:10-14

Context

A word about parables. Parables are stories. Like good stories, they use images and allusions. Sometimes (too often) with the best of intentions, preachers or teachers take parables and tear them apart, applying each element as though it were a recipe or a moral formula. Parables are not recipes nor scientific formulae. Nor are they allegories. They are stories that allude, hint and challenge through their images. Reflecting on the parables of Jesus becomes far more exciting and disturbing for me when I stop 'overthinking' or rationalising them, when I let the images speak.

The starting point for me is to listen to the Word, trying to let the parable speak. I say 'trying' because the very familiarity of the parables can often dull my hearing. That is when a little bit of reading about the context in which Jesus told his story, and how his listeners *might* have heard it can help me reflect on how that parable might speak to me today.[66]

Reflection on the missing

Luke brings the stories of the lost sheep, the lost coin and the lost son together into one three-part parable as Jesus' response to muttered criticism from people who think he should keep better company, avoid eating in public places and certainly avoid 'eating and drinking with sinners'. In each story there is a thanksgiving celebration: more feasting.

Jesus' first response to this criticism is a story about one sheep missing from a whole flock of sheep. What a fine shepherd to know each sheep and to be aware when one has wandered off! This is a story about the one who is missing... and yet remembered by the shepherd who knows each individual whether it is the little lamb, the slow old ram or the pregnant ewe.

Who is missing? Who are the overlooked in our society? Our families? In our workplaces? From our church?

who is missing from the list of contacts in my phone – those I cherish?	who is missing from the welcome to this altar of remembrance and of fellowship?

---

[66] There are many resources on the parables. I was encouraged in my instinct about parables after reading Amy-Jill Levine's entertaining, *Short Stories by Jesus, The Enigmatic Stories of a Controversial Rabbi*, Harper Collins, 2014.

> who is missing
> from this family meal
> where the table
> has no place set
> for any other?

> who is missing
> from the list of those
> approved
> to share their gifts
> in ministry and service?

> who is missing
> from this school
> that teaches
> in the name
> of Jesus?

> who is missing
> from this table
> where decisions
> are being made
> about our future?

4.4c Who's feeling lost around here?

Reading

Mark 6:33-34

Many of us feel a little lost in our societies and communities; some feel totally forgotten. Many of us feel impotent, feel that our voice is being ignored; that those voices calling for greater compassion and humanity often seem overruled by our governments, church, bureaucracies.

> they rush to him,
> women from their pots
> men from their flocks –
> wind tosses dry leaves
> with rumours of something new

The crowds described in Mark 6 are desperate for a leader they can trust, a teacher they can follow, a shepherd who will recognise them, acknowledge them and care for them. For those from around Nazareth listening to him, Jesus was someone they already knew. He was familiar. Yet his response was different.

> a man like them
> who grew up with them –
> knowing them,
> he still reaches out
> with unexpected kindness

God is for all people. The kingdom of God is for everyone, even now.

4.4d What is missing?

Reading

Parable of the lost coin: Luke 15:8-9

Recently, a friend who is an Uber driver received a massive traffic fine, the equivalent of three days' income. He was devastated. He had to put in many extra hours to recoup the loss. We've all lost things that are important to us. For me, it was a small gold earring, one of a pair that my husband gave me just after our marriage. I searched high and low, emptying out my handbag, shining a torch into the corners of cupboards, looking in the same places again and again. Finally, and unexpectedly, I found the earring (or it found me) eighteen months later lodged under piles of leaves in the corner of steps near my sister's front door. I still delight in recalling that find.

In Luke's version of the 'Lost Coin' story, the woman in the story has lost a silver piece. Since she owns only ten silver pieces, this is a significant loss. Sensibly, she searches thoroughly, and gives the house a great unplanned spring-clean to find the missing coin.

Perhaps the silver coin is like the fire enkindled by Jesus' teaching as expressed in the following hymn,

> God whose purpose is to kindle,
> now ignite us with your fire.
> While the earth awaits your burning,
> with your passion us inspire.
> Overcome our sinful calmness,
> stir us with your saving name.
> ...
> Lift the smallness of our vision
> by your own abundant life.[67]

For me the parable raises questions about what might be missing from my life, my family, my workplace, my church, my world.

What is missing

> arms that embrace with tenderness
> gentleness as we walk upon the earth
> spirits as wide and deep as the ocean
> passion to work together to heal country
> attentiveness to those who long for justice
> hope as tenuous and strong as butterfly wings
> voices that decry injustice whoever perpetrates it
> foolishness to imagine the kingdom here and now

---

[67] 'God whose purpose is to kindle,' text Luke 12:49; David E. Trueblood, copyright 1967, David Elton Trueblood; sung to Beethoven's 'Ode to Joy'.

contemplation of the beauty in each moment
days and darkness electrically powered with the Gospel
time spent in the timelessness of the infinite

Let me find them...
then find them again
and again,
I will call up my friends,
we will sing and dance

4.4e Dissension, reconciliation and celebration: parable of a man with two sons

Reading

Luke 15:11-32

Context

A reminder: Luke places this as the third part of Jesus' response to his critics that 'this fellow welcomes sinners and eats with them' – unlike John and his disciples who fast.

Spoiler alert. I am responding to this as a story of a man and his two sons. I am ascribing no identity to anyone in the story other than that of a man and his two male offspring.

A man with two sons

This is the story of a family; a story of things familiar to all of us.

A man has two sons.

And as is the way with many families, there is dissension. One young fellow demands his entitlements and takes off. His father gives in. His elder brother remains. The man's wife and daughters are out of sight. This is about a dad and his adult sons.

The father

he flouts
his duty, this boy of mine,
itching, twitching
against any advice,
he walks away from us

The younger son

harnessed here
like my father's oxen
dumb and dull –
cut me free
I want to live

The elder son

every day
I rise early
oversee servants
toiling in the fields –
tied to my father's house

None of the men is happy.
(Not to mention the women of the family.)

The father

rats scratch,
gnawing in the rafters,
all through the night
regrets about my son
... why I let him go

The younger son	The elder son

whiffs of fresh bread,	as I plough
memories of sleep	the field of my birthright,
in a warm soft bed –	the blade cuts sharply
hungry, smelly, cold...	deep into the furrow –
I can do better than this	my father's disregard

Then, one day, the younger man comes home.

The father

in the courtyard
water overfills the trough
gushing, splashing –
nothing big enough
to hold my happiness

The younger son	The elder son

I've rehearsed	across the fields
my lines, I know	the shrill of flutes,
the part to play –	clank of tambourines –
'Father, I'm not worthy	hollowed out,
to be called your son'	forgotten

There is always time to try to fix the wrongs.

The father

lightning splits
the old oak tree,
scorches its core –
the ferocity
of a parent's love

The younger son	The elder son
such a feast...	the old man
my father outdoes himself	comes and begs me
without a word	join the party –
of disapprobation –	a little late to realise
this is my moment	he has another son

Is this what Jesus meant when he told this story to those who criticised his delight in sharing meals with all and sundry? Was he saying, 'I eat and drink and celebrate a God I know as a father of abundant tenderness, who rejoices when those we thought we'd lost are found again, when those we thought were dead are restored to life and when divisions between us are healed'? And was he also saying, 'I celebrate a God whose foolishly extravagant love is not contingent on how we respond'? The love is there, regardless. Any parent knows this!

4.5 A kingdom for everyone

Reading

Crossing to the other side: Mark 4:35, 7:31, Luke 8:22, Matthew 8:18

Feedings in Roman and Greek areas: Matthew 15:32-39, Mark 8:1-9

Gerasenes: Matthew 8:28-34, Mark 5:1-20, Luke 8:26-39

Healing foreigners: Mark 7:24-30, Matthew 15:21-28, Matthew 8:5-13, Luke 7:1-10, John 4:46-53

Samaritan woman: John 4:1-42

Place

In some ways, it is still 'the other side', the land across the Sea of Galilee, east of the River Jordan. This is the area that reaches up the steep climb of Golan Heights, towards the border with modern Lebanon and occupied Syria. Near the Syrian border, there is a United Nations no-go zone. Remnants of warfare, past and ongoing, are visible along the road: a mosque pockmarked with bullets and mortars, destroyed Muslim Arab villages, rusting Israeli jeeps in fields, the edge of the demilitarised area bristling with communication towers. Signs hanging on the wire fences by the road warn about landmines.

Context

In Jesus' time, first century CE, the 'other side' was an area where Jews were unlikely to go: to the land of the foreigners, such as the cities of the Decapolis and Banias.

In the Gospels, we read of Jesus breaking these boundaries. 'Let us cross to the other side', he said to his disciples more than once.

Mark's Gospel has two feeding stories. Some scholars suggest that the feeding of 5000 with 12 baskets of food remaining (chapter 6) refers to the Gospel reaching the twelve tribes of Israel, while the feeding of 4000 in the foreign area of the Decapolis with seven baskets of food (chapter 8) is referencing Jesus' mission to the Gentiles. Between the two feeding stories, Mark inserts the story of Jesus healing the daughter of a Syrophoenician woman (7:24-30) with its many allusions to feeding and bread. The woman – we need to remember – is a Gentile (an outsider), hence all the repartee about dogs and feeding from crumbs beneath the table.

4.5a The other side

Jesus chooses to extend the feast of abundance to non-Jews, just as he has already shared it with his own people.

> you choose to go
> beyond the expected
> boundaries
> we put up
> with-in our churches

At other times, Jesus stays with Samaritans – certainly not done by Jews; he heals the servant of a Roman official – one of the invading oppressors; he heals the daughter of a Canaanite or Syro-Phoenician woman – a foreigner – who challenges him to respond. He responds to their expressions of faith, belief in him and his word.

> the 'others'
> become 'us'
> this freedom
> to defy convention –
> where is it today?

Jesus healed the demoniac in Gerasenes who was definitely on the other side in every sense, geographically, culturally and psychologically. He had no name – although his demons had a name.

I am with my brother in the emergency department at St Vincent's, but it could be the emergency department of any city hospital. The woman in Bed 5 is thin and malnourished. Fuelled by ice, or some combination of drugs, she is strong beyond her riddled frame. Three police can barely restrain her. She struggles against their determination and the handcuffs on her wrists. Her howling is that of the demented, penetrating through the busy space, already crammed with the pain of the badly injured and dangerously ill.

> from the tombs
> in that desolation
> he emerges
> gaunt, bruised, ranting
> chillingly demonic

What kindness will it take to call out the demons from within the woman in Bed 5? How long have they possessed her? What patience, what persistent love, will it take to bring her to that place where she might sit, calm and clothed? Ready to grow into her true self and to resume her interrupted life?

4.6 Waiting for the kingdom

Reading

Matthew 6:5-15, Luke 11:1-4
Ezekiel 36:23, Daniel 4:32, Proverbs 30:8-9, Isaiah 35:4, 59:19-20,
Romans 8:26-27, 2 Thessalonians 3:3, Ephesians 4:32

Context

The kingdom preached by Jesus is also a future kingdom. God's reign is both recognised here and now and not yet realised. Jesus' preaching points to the end times, to the final coming of God's reign in glory when all will be as it should be in accord with God's will.

As he taught his followers then, he teaches us to pray now...

4.6a Petitions about God

God of the universe, Lord of heaven and earth, Holy One.
    You are our God, and holy is your name.
        Still, we feel free to call you Father,
  Appa, Tatay, Aaba, Tamai, Baba, el Papa, Dad.[68]
Holy God, high above the cosmos, and close to us.

We long for your kingdom to come here on earth so that we can see what your reign in heaven means.
When we see:
- those seeking asylum from oppression exiled into a system of cruelty which turns their hope to bitterness,
- the programs set up with good intent to serve the aged, needy and vulnerable leave them still in need,
- the first peoples of our countries overly represented in poverty, disadvantage and in our prisons,
- nations' leaders unable to put aside political advantage for the common good of their people to govern with justice, compassion and wisdom,

---

[68] *Appa* (Tamil), *Tatay* (Filipino), *Aaba* (Somali), *Tamai* (Tongan), *Baba* (Italian), *el Papa* (Spanish).

- women, men and children sleeping rough in our cities and towns without a place to call their own,
- women and children suffering violence in their own homes,
- men and women losing their lives to addiction,
- priests and others in religion violating their sacred trust towards children and towards you,
- even those who invoke your name unable to put aside the hostilities that break hearts, destroy lives and leave only bitterness and grief,

with all our being, we ache for a future when your world-order is established.

4.6b Petitions for ourselves

Give us our daily bread, the bread we need beyond today...

- save us from the drought which spreads across our land, even if it is of our own making. Give us water to fill our rivers and dams so the fish can flourish in the waters and our crops can be irrigated into sufficiency,
- inspire us to educate our children and young people so that they can face their adult lives with confidence and skills and build up their communities,
- guide us into imaginative ways of working that permit everyone to contribute positively and creatively each in their own way and according to their skills,
- teach us to share from our abundance so that everyone in our society has sufficient for each day, and to share from the wealth of our nation so that all peoples have sufficient for each day now and into the future.

4.6c Petition for forgiveness

We beg to be freed from the heavy weight of our shortcomings, from the burden of the debt of love, as we also pray to be freed from the encumbrance of our anger and resentment against those who have offended us (and who keep on offending), who've overstepped the mark with us (and keep on taking liberties).

We ask forgiveness for...

- taking for granted the gift of life and the wonders of your creation and how we have overstepped the mark (trespassed) in our abuse of the laws of nature,
- being slow to forgive those who are in debt to us... internationally, within our country and between neighbours and in families,
- the need to be forgiven over and over because we are too willing to distrust the capacity you give us for good,
- undervaluing our indebtedness to all those who have fed and clothed, educated and guided us,
- all the ways in which we do not forgive, adding to our indebtedness to you,
- for the land and dignity we have stolen from original inhabitants in many countries,
- our blindness and stubbornness in destroying your gift of Earth and for robbing our children and all creation – your children and your creation – of a sustainable future,
- for locking ourselves in pettiness, for chaining up imagination, and for
- closing our hearts to the new directions your Spirit guides us towards.

4.6d Petition for the future

Lead us not into temptation. Do not test us more than we can cope with.

We ask your help...

- against the ultimate temptation to put our trust only in ourselves and to lose heart,
- for those caged for years in prison, denied access to family and kindness, subject to punishment, squalor and control,
- in raising up our children with all their challenges and demands,
- in caring for our aged,
- to remain always open to leave behind the old and face the new.

And we all say, Amen. We can't wait for your kingdom to come.

Something to think about

Juan Pagola writes that Jesus' fundamental calling was 'to awaken faith in the nearness of God by struggling against suffering... This is the kingdom of God that he yearned for: the defeat of evil, the irruption of God's mercy, the elimination of suffering, the acceptance of those previously excluded from community life, the establishment of a society liberated from all affliction. That is far from being an accomplished reality'.[69]

*

---

[69] Pagola, pages 174, 175.

'While the Church is oriented towards end-times, we also live in 'end-times': our 'now' is the end-time of all that has gone before. Our current world, too, is a place of ambiguity arising from the end-times (*eschata*) of many certainties. Theologian Vitor Westhelle describes the... community of believers as a space of grace in the pointy end of life... Because of the Spirit's presence, 'the place of risk, of condemnation, is also the place of healing and salvation'.[70]

*

Denis McBride writes about 'the lost and the last and the least, whose open woundedness is a cry to the graciousness of God. These are the ones who are hugged into importance by an eccentric king who cherishes them above all others. These are the ones who are surprised by love and beneficence in the parables of the kingdom.'[71]

*

The word used in Matthew 5:3, the Beatitudes, comes from a word meaning to crouch or cower like a beggar, someone who is deeply destitute, bent down, burdened with poverty, one who is poor beyond the poverty of a peasant, depressed, defenceless, totally devoid of resources. While Matthew speaks of 'poor in spirit', the *Jerusalem Bible* indicates that Jesus usually has actual poverty in mind. Not

---

[70] This extract is from Anne Benjamin and Charles Burford, *Leadership in a Synodal Church*, Garratt Publishing, Melbourne, 2021, page 8, quoting Vitor Westelle as quoted in Richard Lennan, 'The Church as Mission: Locating vocation in its ecclesial context' in Christopher Jamison & T. Clark, *The Disciples' Call: Theologies of Vocation from Scripture to the Present Day*, e-book, London, 2013, page 49.

[71] Denis McBride, *Jesus and the Gospels*, Chawton Hampshire, Redemptorist Publications, 2002, page 110.

only are these people poor, but they know it in their bones and empty bellies.

*

'Jesus was not talking abstractly about "poverty", but about the poor whom he met on his travels through the villages. Families that were barely surviving, people who struggled against losing their land and their honour, children threatened by hunger and malnutrition, prostitutes and beggars despised by all, the sick and demon-possessed who were denied even a minimum of dignity, lepers marginalised by their society and religion...'[72]

*

'Something exceedingly good happens to people in their encounter with Jesus Christ.'[73]

---

[72] Pagola, page 112.
[73] Johnson and Rakoczy, page 7.

5
Followers, companions, disciples

Fourth Century Synagogue at Capernaum

5.1 By your friends...

Reading

Psalm 82, Psalm 103

Place

Galilee, Capernaum, Bethsaida, across the Sea in the foreign lands of the Gerasenes, in the off-limits region of Samaria, Bethany near Jerusalem, Jerusalem.

Context

In 1st Century CE region that is now Palestine, there were elites: the military officials, tax collectors, administrators, large landowners. However, most people were poor, '... families who struggled to survive day by day, but at least they had a small piece of land or some stable employment to live on. But when Jesus talks about the *poor*', Pagola continues, 'he is referring those who have nothing: people living on the edge, dispossessed of everything, at the opposite extreme from the powerful elites. The poor live without wealth, without power, and without honour'.[74]

5.1a Grounded in religious memory

Jesus was remembered as seeking out, welcoming and engaging with:

a prophet and his followers

John the Baptiser – scruffy, disturbing, ill-clad, choosing to live in the desert, who insisted on calling people

---
[74] Pagola, page 181.

to repentance and conversion, who was imprisoned and murdered;

poor folk
who ran from towns to see him, unemployed, homeless, transients whom he welcomed with warmth and compassion;

harassed, dejected, rudderless, mentally-disturbed and vulnerable folk
for whom society held no place;

those who were sick and suffering
with no support, guarantees of healing or hope;

those regarded as ritually impure by the religious institution, 'unfit persons',
such as lepers, tax collectors, a woman accused of adultery, women known as sinners;

well-off people
such as Levi and Zacchaeus, possibly the woman with a haemorrhage and the religious leader Jairus and his little girl; such as a rich young man who could not meet the challenge of following him; a woman with ointment in a house in Bethany; Lazarus, Martha and Mary; Joanna and probably Mariam of Magdala; his host who owned the house where he gathered for his last meal with his friends; Joseph of Arimathea and fishermen who ran businesses;

foreigners, the religiously unacceptable, the 'other'
like the poor possessed distressed man in Gerasene, a Syro-Phoenician woman, a Samaritan woman and a Samaritan leper;

the politically incorrect, the oppressors and the rulers
including an official and his son and a Roman Centurion and his servant;

teachers of the law
Pharisees called Nicodemus and Simon; Sadducees, Scribes and Pharisees; and crowds;

children and street kids
who welcomed him without inhibition, unencumbered by 'should' and 'shouldn't';

Jesus seemed to care little for public opinion. He placed himself outside the social mainstream but within the mainstream of those loved by the God of his Jewish tradition.

5.1b His *modus operandi*

His focus is on God his father.
His passion is for those who suffer,
feeling with them viscerally.
Faith is what he looks for and responds to.
He disturbs things and people.
He gives advice on hosting dinners,
who to invite and where to sit,
but he eats and drinks with all and sundry.

Whom do we seek out?
What does this say about our God?

5.2 Being a disciple

5.2a Troubling

I went to collect the dry-cleaning and a parcel from the Post Office. A young woman walked behind my car as I reversed. I thought I might have given her a fright. When I had parked the car, I went and spoke with her, as she sat on a milk crate outside the doctor's surgery. I apologised. She asked me for change. 'Sorry, Dar,' I said, and went across to the dry-cleaner.

I was troubled by the idea of Jesus and how he might respond. If he (meaning me) was *for* those in need, how would he (meaning me) go about it? Talking with her would have been a start.

I was conscious of my distance from her. Yes, I spoke, but I didn't go that extra step and ask a little more or chat, as the old man from the church appeared to do when I saw him later talking to her.

When I came back from the Post Office – clutching, somewhat ironically, James Martin's book on *Jesus* – I saw that she had gone. I felt relief.

I also felt shame as a person who calls herself a disciple of Jesus.

5.2b Discipleship costs

Reading

Costs of discipleship: Luke 9:23-24, 9:57-62, 17:19-23,
Matthew 8:18-22, 10, 16:24-25, John 12:25,
Family rejection: Mark 3:20-22, John 7:5
Rewards of discipleship: Matthew 19:29, Luke 18:29-30
Warnings to his disciples: Matthew 16: 21-33, 20:17-19,
Luke 9:21-22, 43-45, 12:51-53,18: 31-34

If...

If I throw my lot in with him, I'll be seen
to be his follower. It's not the wisest move –
not guaranteed to help me
get ahead. What if
he turns out to be someone
I don't like?
Perhaps he really is a bit odd,
out of his mind? Even his family says that.
He's so determined, there surely is
some abnormality here,
a messiah complex maybe?
After building my life around him
what if I find him
too demanding? Challenging?
Wanting more than I can give?
More than I want to give?
What if I find him too religious

(just when I've been liberated)?
Too focused? Too clear-sighted?
Uncompromising? Too pure in heart?
There's no turning back, no going home,
he warns us, but what if
I find it is too hard to walk with him?
That he asks too much of me –
and I walk away?
What then?
How will I see myself then?

5.2c The challenge of following him

Reading

Mark 8:22-10:52
   Instructions to his disciples:

- From blindness to sight: 8:22-26
- 'Peter, stop making it harder': 8:31-33
- The cross and disciples: 8:34-9:1
- Transfiguration and the cross: 9:2-13
- Need for prayer, time with God: 9:14-29
- Service, openness, humility: 9:33-10:31
- Cross and servanthood: 10:32-45
- From blindness to sight: 10:46-52

Context

Jesus chose very deliberately the people he wanted as his disciples.

In the Gospels, the first-generation Christians – those with living memory – portrayed Jesus as someone who was uncompromising in his expectations of his followers. The Gospel of Mark, in chapters 8:22 to 10:52, gathers together some of Jesus' instructions to his disciples. The Gospel bookends these instructions with stories of sight being given to the blind... a message to the disciples who couldn't see and now begin to see.

Reflection

If you choose to follow this man,

>be prepared to
>do it now
>do it wholeheartedly
>to let go of your moorings
>keep going out into the deep
>be mentally itinerant, a constant missionary
>lose the approval of your family and friends
>be ridiculed and criticised
>possibly lose your career
>(and hopes of making a fortune)
>find yourself in solitariness
>find yourself with all sorts of people
>in all sorts of places
>and having to hang on in
>
>as you walk every step with joy.

5.2d Salt

As salt is to tastelessness and antiseptic to wounds
As light is to darkness
As the true north of principle is to expedience
As forgiveness is to rifts between us
As fidelity is to marriage and friendship
As truth is to shiftiness
As peacemaking is to violence
As love is to those who despise us
As generosity is to the poor
As prayer is to the search for one's self
As things of the spirit are to the ephemeral
As trust in Providence is to anxiety
As acceptance is to those who offend
As seeking is to one's sense of direction
As respect is to oneself
As kindness is to the hurting
As wisdom is to the phony...
This is how it is to be his disciple.

5.3 Who took up his challenge?

5.3a Women took up the challenge

Reading

Luke 8:1-3

Place

All over Galilee, at the Last Supper, by the cross, at the tomb and in the upper room.

Context

According to the evangelists, and supported by scholars, many women travelled with Jesus, committing themselves to his mission. Some, we are told, had been cured of evil spirits and infirmities. Others were women of status and of wealth. They included: Mariam of Magdala, Joanna (wife of Chuza), Mary (wife of Clopas), Susanna, Salome (mother of James and John), Mary (mother of James the Younger) and many others. Some were there with their sons; some might have been accompanying their husbands.

Reflection

They must be quite determined women. What convinces them to risk the scandal of sleeping on the road as they follow a single man around the countryside? It isn't every day that women such as this travel like this, especially as Jesus is getting a reputation about the kind of people he eats and drinks with.

Take Joanna. She is a woman of wealth and standing. Her husband, after all, manages Herod's household, a responsible position, that gives her access to the royal palace and its people. Despite her position, she too has her difficulties, and an illness plagues her.

No doubt, Chuza, Joanna's husband, with his proximity to his employer, has observed Herod's fascination with John the Baptiser: simultaneously perplexed by the wild-looking John and wanting to listen to him. We can imagine how Joanna's husband might share this with her. Does this lead to him mentioning the other prophet of whom John speaks? A man called Jesus who is making a name for himself as a healer? Do she and her husband discuss the possibility that she might get some relief from her ailment from John or from this new teacher, Jesus? Or does Joanna decide this alone?

Whatever transpired, there is a day, an hour, a place, when Joanna acts decisively. She goes out from the palace to find and meet Jesus.

Does she send a palace worker to find out where she'll meet him? How does she approach Jesus, this woman of means? She stands out in the crowd around him for her dress, her bearing, her manner of speech. How does the encounter take place? What does she say? How does she ask for help? For healing?

For Joanna, it is monumental.

Experiencing that she is healed, and despite all her connections and their concomitant constraints, she chooses to join the group who accompany Jesus. How is she received in the band of Jesus' followers – this member of the royal household? Do the men accept her immediately? Or does she have to earn her credibility? Along with Mariam of Magdala, Susanna and others with means, she offers practical support to keep the band of disciples fed and housed. The practical support of their money and resources (and resourcefulness) buoys up the other followers... a very committed statement of confidence in Jesus' authenticity and significance. Their contributions help sustain the disciples on the road.

Does she become one of the earliest teachers? Like Jesus himself, she crosses to the 'other side' as she moves between her life on the road and the palace. As she speaks with her husband and with other members of the palace household, what does she share about her time with Jesus? About his teaching?

At the end, she is there as Jesus suffers, accompanying him into his death.

And in the dawn of Easter, she is there again, rising early to anoint his body, but instead becoming, with Mariam of Magdala, one of the first witnesses to his life beyond death. Once more, like Mariam, she needs to convince the men who do not believe them, who ridicule them, 'You women, you're imagining things. His tomb is empty? Such a tall tale. Stop disturbing us with this nonsense, women. Stick to your cooking pots'.

Did she then glance sideways at Mariam, raise her eyebrows and shrug her shoulders as though to say, 'Men...'?

5.3b Mariam of Magdala took up the challenge

Context

Magdala was a city near the Sea of Galilee not far from Tiberias. It was famous for fish-salting. In the first century CE, it was large enough to have a large and decorated synagogue. Scholars debate whether Jesus visited Magdala or not, but it is certainly within the area he frequented in his ministry.

One early disciple whom Jesus had cured of 'seven demons', Mariam became a significant witness to the resurrection and played a key role in the early community of believers. (There is absolutely no reason to believe she was a prostitute.)

She might have come from Magdala or 'Magdala' might have been a nickname Jesus gave her. As one scholar has suggested, *Migdal* is a Hebrew word that 'refers to a tower or enclosure to hold fish under water. It was also used to refer to a tower in a vineyard or shepherd's field for spotting danger. Both usages stress the notion of holding together and strength'.[75] I rather like this reading.

Mariam's response

Have you ever been out of your mind? I mean, totally out of control? When I first met him, I had no centre: ranting and tormented by night, paralysed by fear and obsessions by day. My poor family had long given up on me. There were times when the braying of a hundred donkeys crashed through my mind; and times when I opened my mouth to speak, that rattling noises escaped, making no sense.

one day he came
and stood before me
speaking
to the furies inside me
Peace, he said.

---

[75] Dr Debra Snoddy, 'Mary Magdalene: The Apostle to the Apostles', *Plenary Post*, 15 March 2020, Plenary Council, https://mailchi.mp/4e358843ec57/plenary-post-edition-15-march-8-2583085

So I began to follow him, drink in his words. We are a motley bunch – but we are held together by the attraction he holds over us and our thirst to understand him more. The men can be so querulous at times. Quite thick, some of them. Arguing over who is best among them, who's closest to him, who deserves his favour more. Sometimes, he'll turn and say, *What do you think, Mariam?* I understand why he slips away at evening to be himself, to rest into the quiet.

> he took away
> my pain and so I follow
> his words
> about a god of love
> make me want to stay

He gives us nicknames, Magdala, Cephas, Boanerges.

> we move slowly
> day after day
> learning
> the freedom to shift
> with his spirit

These have been wonderful years. The best of my life. I could not have imagined living like this, on the road, moving from place to place with Joanna, Susanna, Salome, James' mum and all the other wives and women, providing for the daily needs of Jesus. We are a community of disciples, sisters and brothers with him.

> this morning I hear
> larks tinkle as they flutter
> so freely
> he gives me a whole new world
> singing with compassion

5.3c People of means and status took up the challenge

Reading

Zacchaeus: Luke 19:1-10,
Lazarus: John 11,12:1-2,
Last Supper host: Mark 14:13-15
Simon the Leper: Mark 14:3, Matthew 25:6

Place

Archaeologists have uncovered evidence of settlement in Jericho dating from around 10,000 BCE, making it possibly the oldest city in human civilisation, at some point known as the City of Palms.

Modern Jericho is a Palestinian city in the West Bank, northeast of Jerusalem. In the April of my visit, glare from the parched, dusty landscape burnt into my eyes.

Being about 26 kilometres from Jerusalem, Jericho was a natural staging point for pilgrims visiting Jerusalem on a route that avoided passing through Samarian territory. Jesus probably passed through Jericho more than once.

It is mountainous, isolated and inhospitable terrain. Its desolation makes an apt setting for the story of the Good Samaritan, and people in first century CE who heard this story would not have been surprised to learn of the traveller being mugged along the way. The mugging, of course, was not the surprise that the story carried. Tourist guides point out a sprawling sycamore tree as the tree Zacchaeus climbed. Our more scholarly guide was a little more ambivalent.

Zaccheus: disciple of impulsiveness and decisiveness

Jesus is on his way to Jerusalem and he passes through Jericho. As a senior tax collector, Zacchaeus would have been unpopular, an agent of the rich and powerful.

How is it that Zacchaeus is so anxious to see the man Jesus whom he's heard about? He's been good at his job. So good that he's become wealthy enough to offer to repay anyone he *might* have cheated four hundred percent. So, what attracts him? What does he expect to get from seeing him? Is Zacchaeus used to acting precipitately?

Whatever its source, some urge drives Zacchaeus to see for himself this person who is causing a lot of fuss and rumour. In his curiosity, he forgets his dignity: he runs as fast as his short legs will take him, charges through the crowd and, God help us, climbs a tree for a better view of Jesus and his fellow-travellers.

> up a sycamore
> on one of my impulses
> like a fool
> is this another moment
> for my mortification

Does he have a flash back as he sits in the tree waiting, peering down through the leaves? Does he recall the stories he has heard about Jesus: sees a gap between that and his own life? Is this a moment of truth for Zacchaeus that he has longed for unconsciously, but hasn't given himself time for?

> every day
> I hurtle to work
> building a life
> I'm too rushed to live
> to see who I'm becoming

Do people on the roadway (some of whom he might have cheated) laugh at him? Jeer? Toss a few sharp stones his way? Is Zacchaeus providing a side-show to the main event? Is this why Jesus looks up and sees him?

Does Jesus laugh? It is, after all, a ridiculous situation. Does Jesus catch Zacchaeus' eye and tease him just a little before he speaks? *What are you doing up that tree, Zacchaeus? You don't have to be so desperate to see me. I'm here now. Come on down. Let's go to your place and spend some time together.*

> when we meet
> he calls me
> by my name –
> as though we are old friends
> as though he accepts me

Zacchaeus has heard enough about this man to know he's disposed towards the poor, and for some reason he probably cannot fathom, he desperately wants to be acceptable to Jesus.

> poised on a branch
> struggling for balance
> he throws down a line
> ... money for the poor
> making-up in excess

People complain, of course. They're critical. Why does Jesus favour this man – and *not us* is what they really mean? *He's off to a sinner's house.* Again.

5.4 Joining his team

5.4a He sends us out

Reading

Sending the Twelve: Luke 9:1-6, Matthew 10:5-42, Mark 6:7-13,
Sending the 72: Luke 10:1-24

> He's sending us
> men and women out
> to speak about him
> carrying nothing spare.
>
> His words are stern –
> don't waste time
> keep going
> spread the word,
>
> don't trouble closed minds,
> just those longing
> for a word of mercy,
> kindness.
>
> After all, that is
> his message –

his core intent —
his business plan:

God is
a mothering father
who feels for us,
welcomes us as we are.

And don't be afraid,
you'll be alright
under the gaze
of your watchful Dad,

your God who looks out
for you — even more
diligently than a woman
cares for her child.

If they don't want
to hear this
tender theology,
then

shake off the dust
and leave, he says —
Even if it is my friend,
my folks, someone I love?

He sees more in me than I do
— but I'll go.

5.4b People Fishers[76]

young men
filling the train carriage
with fishing gear,
slabs of beer and banter –
what news do they want?

on a park bench
two old sun-hardened salts
prepare to sleep
under the stars –
how might they respond?

lean cyclist
with tangled dark curls
and a whiff of sea
and brine, and sneakers –
how might he respond?

young girls
sauntering with bare legs
and sauciness
along the harbour walk –
what good news do they bring?

in a thick warm fleece,
a Tongan fisherman
sets up tackle for the night
on the breakwater –
who might he catch?

---

[76] Reflections during a visit to Newcastle, NSW.

5.5 The Twelve

Reading

Establishing the Twelve: John 1:35-51, Matthew 10:2-4, 19:28, Mark 3:13-21, Luke 16:12-16, Acts 1:12-26, 1 Corinthians 15:3-5
Fishers of men: Luke 5:1-11, Mark 1:14-20, Matthew 4:18-22, John 1:40-42
Sons of Thunder: Luke 9:54,
Disputes: Matthew 18:1-5, 20:20-28, Mark 10:35-45, Luke 9:46-50
Don't be afraid: Matthew 10:26-31, Luke 12:4-12, 22-32

Place

Around Galilee.

Context

The early Christians reported that Jesus chose twelve who formed his inner circle, not just as a symbol of the Twelve Tribes of Israel, but as a prophetic enactment of the coming of God's reign in Israel. Scholars refer to Jesus' eschatological orientation – towards the realisation of God's coming in the end times. He formed the Twelve to model discipleship and then sent them out as prophetic missionaries to their own nation.

With some variations between evangelists, the Twelve appear to have been: brothers Simon Cephas and Andrew who were fishermen, and Andrew's friends Philip and Bartholomew from Bethsaida; James and John, whose father Zebedee had a fishing business; Alpheus' son James and Jacob's son Jude. Matthew (not a tax collector), Thomas, Judas Iscariot and the Canaan Simon.

5.5a Why did they say 'yes'

What made Simon and Andrew say yes to him? Something more than John the Baptiser's endorsement. Something in Jesus himself. What was it that convinced them to leave their work for others to complete? For Simon to leave his home, and, perhaps, even to persuade his wife to join him in an itinerant life?

> surprising
> the way he played
> with the word –
> *come with me, keep fishing...*
> *but catch men not 'musht'*[77]

Why did the brothers James and John say yes to him? Men with a family business, men whose family had given them expectations about their prospects. With a mother who assumed they would do well in the kingdom Jesus announced.

---

[77] *Musht*: fish, specifically, tilapia, a fish promoted to contemporary tourists in Galilee as 'Peter's fish', whether or not it actually was the fish Cephas and Andrew were catching. I am taking a little poetic licence here.

> their voices
> boom from boat to boat,
> *boanerges,*
> wanting fire and revenge –
> it's not that kind of kingdom

Why did the Canaan Simon say *yes* to his invitation? A man known to be zealous about honouring the Law and its rubrics.

> all my life
> I've observed the rules
> practised my faith
> but to him
> that's not enough:
>
> last night again
> we ate and drank and talked
> for hours, with him
> I find myself companion
> to those I thought unfaithful

Why did Judas Iscariot say *yes* to his invitation? The Twelve and the group of other disciples live in fellowship, supported by friends, meals prepared in common, helped, no doubt, by the women. Judas looks after the finances which they pool for their needs.

> did anyone notice
> I found a way to stretch
> our money
> yet again, so we could eat?
> we need a business plan –
>
> instead, he gestures
> at the yellow buttercups
> and hopping sparrows,
> dips his bread into the dish
> ... says, *don't worry*

5.5b Friction in the camp

The Twelve and their companions are drawn together by this man, but they bring into the intimacy of their life on the road their disparate capacities, the confines of their own experiences and personalities, their different understandings of what he is teaching.

In choosing the Twelve who would be his closest friends, Jesus probably focused on attributes other than refinement, education, an easy-going temperament, personal hygiene and dress sense. These things would have impacted them in the closeness of their days and nights together.

> one day
> a woman asks a favour
> for her sons –
> why does she think
> they warrant privilege
>
> he rebukes
> both righteous anger
> and ambition –
> *if you want to be great*
> *you must be a servant*

5.5c Time for a break

Reading

Matthew 14:1-12, Mark 6:14-29, Luke 9:1-9

Place

Perhaps Bethsaida.

Invitation to rest

The women and men come back from their journeys, full of stories about their teaching. *Come away,* Jesus said to them, *let's go somewhere quiet.* Of course, when they got there, the crowds were there again – just when the disciples wanted to be alone, to talk amongst themselves, to make sense of things – and, of course, Jesus attended to the crowds of people first.

Imagine hearing those words... *Come away where it's quiet, all by ourselves. Let's rest awhile.*

We do it, don't we? List all we've done. All we're doing constantly. The demands upon our time and mind. Repeated like a mantra we can't stop. Aloud or playing in our heads. It is undeniably good work – our work in hospital wards, work in offices, caring for our families, our work in classrooms and after-school initiatives, our spare time spent in voluntary work, our commitment to public service as a political representative, our efforts as parents. Yet underneath the litany of activity some questions niggle us about its meaning, its value, the 'why' of it all. What difference is it making? Our lifestyles can be terrible: long days, late nights, late meals taken on the run; or worse, public function meals of greasy quiche and mini-meat pies. Meals standing, each one taken with a different group, *All hail fellow, well met,* but little continuity of fellowship.

Come and get some rest. The invitation recognises us. The invitation goes beyond what we have and do, and beyond what others want, and take, from us. The invitation reaches each of us. With all our higher ideals, confused desires, self-interest and generosity, weariness and the need to know our efforts matter, that our efforts are meaningful, that we matter.

Come and get some rest. No comments on our performance, no chiding for poor effort, no praise for diligence. We are trusted to make those self-assessments for ourselves.

Only the recognition that we are wearied. And something else, even more precious, making himself available to spend that time with us.

> our boat moves
> with the swell
> towards the promise
> of the other shore
> shifting our perspectives

Mark's Gospel might have said that Jesus sent the apostles away, *Go home to your families, now. Take a day, a few days, off. Get some rest.* That would have been a kind and sensitive gesture. Instead, Jesus gave the Twelve something far more attentive and complimentary, *Come with me, just us, to a quiet place and get some rest.* He wanted to be with them in an uncrowded place, away from people, for the moment.

The affection implied in such an invitation is restorative. It needed to be, because the quiet escape that he proposed to his apostles (like many of our own) would not last long.

> on the water
> waves thump the hull –
> in his company
> we breathe in the wind
> see things more clearly

5.5d Simon Cephas – Peter

Reading

Simon Peter as spokesperson for the Twelve: Mark 1:36, 10:28, Matthew 15:15, 17:24, 18:21, Luke 12:41, 22:7-13, John 6:68
Jesus prays for Peter: Luke 22:31-32
Peter's denial: Luke 22:54-62, Matthew 26:69-75, Mark 14:66-72, John 18:15-18, 25-27
Peter's confession of faith: Matthew 16:13-20, Mark 8:27-30, Luke 9:18-20, John 6:67-69
Jesus predicts his suffering and death: Matthew 16:21-28, 17:9-13
Jesus rebukes Peter: Matthew 16:21-28, Mark 8:31-34

Place

Around Galilee, in nearby mountains and deserted places, in Caesarea Philippi.

Caesarea Philippi is about 44 kilometres north of Capernaum. It is a place charged with significance as the source of the Jordan River emerging from the melted snows on Mount Hermon. An enormous cave bears evidence of ancient pagan worship to the Greek god Pan and signs of an early city known as Banias (Panias).

The Gospels do not identify on which mountain the experience recorded as the transfiguration occurred. Nor does it matter. The place today remembered as the place of the transfiguration is Mount Tabor. It is accessed by a steep and winding road, well worth the effort of the climb because of the peacefulness and beauty of the gardens, cathedral and monastery that have been built there. As in other places of Christian pilgrimage in Israel, the mosaics and murals are inspiring.

Context

The synoptic Gospels imply that Jesus made Simon Cephas and the two Zebedee men his inner group, his 'executive'. They were there when he cured Jairus' daughter, on the mountain of transfiguration and in the garden the evening before his death. In Luke, Jesus sends Peter and John ahead to set-up for the Passover celebrations for their group.

Simon Cephas tended to become a spokesperson for the Twelve. At some stage, he reached a point of insight and conviction about the significance of Jesus: this man he had chosen to follow for the past couple of years; with whom he had shared nights and days, crowds and isolation, dusty roads and nights sleeping outdoors or in caves.

Mark and Matthew's Gospels place Simon Peter's dramatic profession of faith in the region of Caesarea Philippi, perhaps highlighting the end of an old pagan cult and the creation of something new in Jesus: Jesus' teaching was not only for individuals, but about the coming of God's kingdom for all of Israel.

In Luke 9:18-20, Jesus is alone with disciples and asks them the big question: 'What are people saying about me?' It is an understandable question, seeking feedback about his impact. Luke's Gospel, typically, has Peter's big reply, his profession that Jesus is the Messiah, occurring when Jesus has been alone praying and in the context of Jesus moving determinedly towards Jerusalem.

Peter speaks out for us all

We meet, as arranged at Bethsaida, full of ourselves, after being on the road, talking about him to people. We were confident in talking about what we'd seen him do, and the words he's said. Not yet quite sure about what it all means.

Amid the chatter, someone brings news about John's murder. It hangs over us... this is someone we know, someone some of us have followed.

> sadness slows us,
> we keep repeating
> words of shock and fear
> being his disciple
> can be deadly serious

We are alone, quieter, away from the people, here in the hills, reflective. Jesus sits at some distance, deep into that other space he enters – praying. After a while, he joins us and starts chatting with us about our journeys teaching about him.

'When you were amongst the villages', he asks, 'what were people saying about me? Did they say who they thought I was?'

'A man asked me if you were John the Baptiser back from the dead', someone said. Others nodded. 'Or that you were a prophet', someone else said. 'Yes', a few of us agreed. 'They thought you might be Elijah or Jeremiah.'

And Jesus looked at us then, steadily, and asked, 'What about you? You've been with me all this time? You've seen what I've been doing, heard what I've been teaching. Who do you think I am?'

There was a pause for a while. And then, Simon Peter settled himself, faced Jesus and said very deliberately, 'I think you are the holy one of God, the one we've been waiting for, God's own son'.

> the breeze
> breathes a hurricane
> through the oak leaves
> words carve open
> a chasm of silence

He is pleased with Simon Peter's answer. He plays with Simon's name, makes puns about rocks and foundations, but he is deadly earnest. He speaks about how he must go to Jerusalem and face what the authorities will hand out to him. Their opposition has been growing. He tells us to expect that he will be killed.

Simon Peter can't accept that. He jumps up and pulls Jesus aside. He is unable to keep the hoarse urgency from his voice. 'This can't happen', Simon tells Jesus. 'This can't happen to you.'

Jesus really turned on him. He raised his voice. He was sterner than I've ever seen him. I think Simon Peter was shocked by his response. 'Get out of my sight. Don't tempt me, don't make it harder than it is. This is something that I must do. I am going to Jerusalem. I must go. If you are serious about what you just said about who I am, then you will follow me. This is not just some ordinary venture we're on. This is godly business.'

the establishment
advises caution –
heed your heart
if you really want
to follow me

my house
needs no marble walls,
no shrine
shored up with scaffolding
or legal certitudes

the wind blusters
through the window holes –
this fragile dwelling
shelter enough
for those who walk with me

5.5e Finally getting the message

Reading

Matthew 17:1-13, Mark 9:2-8, Luke 9:28-36, 51-56

One night, Jesus takes Simon Peter, James and John away to spend the night with him in the hill area nearby. Maybe they go to pray together; maybe to talk through the threats against Jesus; maybe to plan some practicalities.

last night
something must have happened
on the mountain
something buoys them up –
he sets out towards Jerusalem

Our group is different now. Subdued. Less querulous. Nervous, but determined. Now Jesus speaks more often of his death as if it is imminent. There are so many moments I want to remember, and not forget, like that time – that powerful moment – when he prayed for Simon Peter.

> I have prayed
> for you my friend –
> may your faith become
> a towering mountain
> a giant karri tree
>
> I have prayed
> for you, my friend
> and for your faith –
> a river filled to the brim
> to refresh those you love

5.5f Too hard

Reading

John 6:60-71

Context

'After this, many of his disciples left him and stopped going with him.'

Reflection

Anyone who has held a leadership position, or who has taken a stand on a matter of principle, knows loneliness:

- The principal who offers a fresh start and forgiveness to a troubled student can face harsh criticism from her staff.
- The mother who leaves the seeming security of a family home for the sake of her children's safety and well-being knows she risks financial insecurity and hardship.
- The religious leader who goes against the tide for the sake of a Gospel of love and respect can feel alienated from his or her peers.
- The whistle-blower who speaks up against corruption or abuse of some kind can find themselves unemployed and unsupported.
- The parent, the team leader, the CEO who tries to discern the best way forward can spend long lonely nights.

Companionship in leadership is a blessing we cannot take for granted:

- The hardest questions are those we ask ourselves: when we question going out on a limb for a principle or person; when we question our investment in a venture or person; when we question why we lent our name to an ideal; when we question what we fundamentally believe; when we wonder if we are reckless and foolish to follow our heart.
- When our friends can no longer walk with us, it can be a very dark night.

At the very time that Jesus intuits the dangers that lie ahead for him, many of his own followers walk away. They would not have been silent. They would have taken their knowledge of the life of the group along with their own fresh doubts and criticisms. He would know that they would talk about him.

How was it for Jesus then?

Something to think about

Peter and Paul 'were not *admirers*, but *imitators* of Jesus. They were not spectators, but rather protagonists of the Gospel. They believed not in words, but in deeds. Peter did not speak about mission, he lived the mission, he was a fisher of men; Paul did not write learned books, but letters of what he lived as he travelled and bore witness. Both spent their lives for the Lord and for their brothers and sisters. And they provoke us, because we run the risk of stalling at the first question: of giving views and opinions, of having grand ideas and saying beautiful words, but never putting ourselves on the line.

And Jesus wants us to put ourselves on the line. How often, for example, we say that we would like a Church that is more faithful to the Gospel, closer to the people, more prophetic and missionary, but then, in practice, we do nothing! It is sad to see that many speak, comment and debate, but few bear witness. Witnesses do not lose themselves in words, but rather they bear fruit. Witnesses do not complain about others and the world, but they start with themselves. They remind us that *God is not to be demonstrated, but shown*, by one's own witness; not announced with proclamations but witnessed by example. This is called 'putting your life on the line'.[78]

---

[78] Pope Francis, 'Solemnity of the Holy Apostles Peter and Paul', Angelus, St Peter's Square, 29 June 2021.

6
Signs of Wonder

Looking across the Sea of Galilee towards Capernaum

6.1 Signs on the sea

Reading

Psalm 107, especially vs 23-32
Mark 4:35-41, Matthew 8:23-27, Luke 8:22-25
Mark 6:45-52, Matthew 14:22-33, John 6:16-21

Context

In chapter 4 of Mark's Gospel, Jesus and the disciples are in a boat in a frightening storm. Jesus sleeps on soundly until his companions panic and wake him. Jesus commands the storm to cease, leaving his followers to wonder 'Who is this, that even wind and sea obey him?'

This first storm incident in Mark precedes a story involving the feeding of 5000 people. Soon after this, there is another incident involving a storm (Mark 6). In this second occurrence of Jesus calming the waters, he is not in the boat, and comes to the disciples' assistance across the turbulent sea. He chides them for their hard-headedness. *Hard-heartedness* is used in one translation. The *Jerusalem Bible* translation says the disciples were *utterly and completely dumbfounded* and their *minds were closed*. I suspect their minds were simply blank.

6.1a Yacht Race

I have spent many Boxing Day mornings watching the start of the Sydney to Hobart Yacht Race on tv. On one occasion, my family and I watched the race at close quarters. The viewing was memorable for me – and not just because it was somewhat curtailed by my being newly pregnant with twins. The flotilla of yachts curved across the water towards the Heads, their sails bent with wind under a near-cloudless sky.

Identifying the maxi-yachts was simple: their logo and sponsors blazoned on their mainsails in huge letters.

To me, this is my image of Mark's story in chapter 4. Jesus sleeps on a cushion, relaxed, at rest. He has no reason for concern, even though the boat is beginning to rise and fall, to thump against the waves, to toss from side to side, losing its momentum.

If most Australians hear the words 'jumbuck', 'coolabah' and 'billabong', there's a likely chance, they'll – subconsciously at least – associate it with the song 'Waltzing Matilda' because the song is so ingrained in our memories and popular culture. In Mark 4:35-41 (and again in Mark 6.45-52), there's a cluster of words that would have offered touchstones to the disciples' knowledge of the psalms, especially Psalm 107: 'tempest', 'waves', 'distress', 'still', 'calm'. In Psalm 107, it is God who hushes waves and still storms – no-one else: only God.

For me, Mark is saying to his community of early believers, that Jesus was giving his disciples a sign about who he was: a sign as clear as if it were painted in gigantic letters on their boat's mainsail. The disciples remained unable (unwilling or too thick) to make that acknowledgment. It was, let's face it, an enormous step.

'What about you?' Mark challenges his community. 'Are your minds closed too?' And us now...

6.1b Who stills the storm?

As experienced fishermen who had spent their lives on the Sea of Galilee, I'm sure Peter and his mates could read the waters and the weather and recognise signs of approaching storms. They would also have handled their boats many times when the sea was rough. Perhaps this storm was worse than any they had encountered.

Or perhaps the story is really about something more...

'Who is this man,
Who is this,
that even
wind and sea obey him?'
there can only be one answer

you read clouds
adjust your sail
to winds –
listen to the psalm
what does it say:

who lifts the waves
into a mighty tempest?
who stills the storm
into a whisper?
there is only One

I stagger, lost,
am frightened and alone –
your Word
mutes turmoil to a whisper
calms the storm of my distress[79]

6.2 Signs of abundance

Reading

Feeding of 5000: Mark 6:32-44, Matthew 14:13-21, Luke 9:10-17, John 6:1-15, 22-60
Feeding of 4000: Mark 8:1-9, Mathew 15:32-39

---

[79] Adapted from Psalm 107.

Place

Feeding 5000: A deserted place, presumably in Galilee.
Feeding 4000: Desert, possibly in the region of the Greek cities of Decapolis.

Context

All four Gospels include at least one of the stories about remarkable community events involving the sharing of food. In both cases, an abundance of food remains.

In Mark 8, the second event is followed 'immediately' by the Pharisees asking for a sign from heaven, another story about the disciples 'forgetting to bring bread' and still 'not getting' what Jesus is about. Jesus, like many an exasperated teacher and parent, asks: *Are you deaf? Are you blind?* Mark follows with the story of the healing of blind man at Bethsaida, having already inserted a story about healing a deaf mute in chapter 7. Then, Peter 'sees', and Mark follows with Peter's profession, 'You are the Messiah'. Finally, Peter seems to have 'got it'. Or almost.

In John's Gospel (chapter 5), the feeding story follows a long discourse in which Jesus addresses the relationship between himself and the Father, explicitly linking himself with Moses. John links this event to the Passover festival, and hence the Jewish memory of the Passover. In John 6, Jesus calls himself the 'bread of life', a step too far, as we have seen, for some of his own disciples, who leave the group and are no longer able to walk with him (John 6:66).

What are Mark's chapters 6 and 8 telling us?

6.2a Memories of abundance

every day
for forty wandering years
they found food
sufficient for the journey
their God in the desert[80]

a widow's
meagre cup of flour
a jug of oil
filled to overflowing –
memory of a prophet[81]

as they ate
he took a piece of bread,
gave thanks,
broke it, sharing
his whole life with them[82]

from the beginning
they came together
breaking bread
shared still fresh
their memories of him[83]

---

[80] cf. Exodus 16.
[81] cf. 1 Kings 17:8-16.
[82] cf. Mark 14:22.
[83] cf. Acts 2:42, 20:7 et al.

6.2b A disciple learns a lesson in hospitality

It was a day of demands and discovering what we didn't know. He'd sent us out, without him, to teach and heal as he does. There'd been little time to eat or rest and we were tired. When we returned, eager to tell him what we'd done, we found him distressed about John's murder. 'Come away', he said, 'let's get away from all this'.

> in my mind
> I'm already there
> out of town
> across the water
> finding peace and quiet

We might have guessed the crowds would find us. They were there, ahead of us, waiting.

> on the shore
> so many people milled
> in circles
> looking lost –
> sheep without a shepherd

He moved among them, spending time with different groups. He listened to them, answered them with stories and soft words. He bent and laid his hand on cripples, old men, a child wrapped up in rags.

Then Peter said, 'Don't you think it's time they went home. They need to eat. Besides, you need a break. We need a break.'

'Feed them, then', he said. We began to count the heads – tens, hundreds, thousands.

being business-like,
prudent with our funds
we counted costs –
he counted on us
giving food till all were filled

we shared
a few fish and loaves
... each one there
marvelling
at the abundance

6.2c Not counting the cost

'Half a year's wages! Do you expect us to spend that much on them?'

· Sunday afternoon. My friend of many years had died just three hours before – too young, too quickly. The lunchtime guest from overseas had left and the house was finally quiet. Feeling a little unwell with a cold and heavy with sadness, I turned off my phone and had just laid down to rest when the doorbell rang. I wanted to ignore the bell... I knew it would be someone needing my husband's attention and assistance...

· To find a more humane response to those in need... How many letters to politicians will it take? How many meetings to attend? How many reports detailing hard evidence must be read? When is it enough?

· That sixteen-year-old girl dotted with piercings and spiky with outrage. Do I have any patience left for her? Do I even know how to handle her?

> from our meagreness
> he asks us to give
> recklessly
> with generosity
> all will be satisfied

'What is that amongst so many?'

Since the COVID-19 pandemic of 2020 and the bushfires of 2019-2020, more of us have a better sense of how it feels to be short of essentials for life. We've experienced how our instinct for survival prompts us to stock up, to be prepared.

Being prepared is prudent. When we give into our fears, it is easy to panic ourselves, so prudence becomes hoarding. Trusting that God gives us talents, imagination and resources sufficient for the needs of the world makes it easier for us to share, not count the cost, see the other as oneself, feel connected in community, to hand over our concerns.

> the lavishness
> of a loving God
> surprises us
> in the desert places
> of our lives

6.2d A God of abundance

> what do we have
> to face a ghostly plague
> and coming death?

> what do we have
> to face the ravages
> and drones of war?

what do we have
to counteract
our private fears?

what do we have
against the tumble
down into despair?

what do we have
to convert politics
to compassion?

what do we have
to reform social process
towards the more humane?

what do we have
to fill the space grief carves?
to melt mounds of guilt?

what do we have
to heal the wound
in Mother Earth?

what do we have
for hungry homeless?
children born in war?

what do we have
for welcome for broken lives
in splintered boats?

what do we have
to shelter women
and children of abuse?

> we have so little –
> yet we hold a memory
> of fish and five small loaves,
>
> of giving thanks, of blessing,
> breaking, sharing... gathering
> baskets of abundance

6.3 Exorcism

Reading

Epileptic Boy: Mark 9:14-29, Matthew 17:14-21, Luke 9:37-43

Place

Somewhere in Galilee.

Context

In Mark, Jesus comes upon a debate between his followers and some men who taught about the Mosaic Law and its interpretation. The followers of Jesus have been unable to cure a boy who is suffering from an affliction of the spirit. The boy's father asks for Jesus' assistance to cure his son and there is a discussion back and forth between them about the boy's condition. The father expresses his faith in Jesus who commands the spirit to leave the boy. The boy falls into a convulsive fit, rolling around, until he is so still the onlookers think he is dead. Then Jesus takes him by the hand, lifts him and the boy stands, cured.

The healing is inserted in all three Synoptics immediately after Peter, James and John's experience of the Transfiguration. Jesus has already begun sharing his intuition that his teaching was leading him into danger with authorities – a hint that the disciples either don't want to hear (Matthew 16:21-23, Mark 8:31-33, Luke 9:21-22) or don't grasp (Matthew 17:22-23, Mark 9:30-32, Luke 9:43b-45).

Mark adds an interesting little incident later in chapter 9 in which John complains to Jesus that he and some disciples had tried to stop someone else who was 'casting out demons' in Jesus' name (Mark 9:38-40). Jesus assured him – maybe with wry humour – not to worry: if the man is acting in Jesus' name now, he certainly won't be able to criticise him later.

Elsewhere, Mark recounts an exorcism of a demoniac in the synagogue in Capernaum (Mark 1:23-28 paralleled in Luke 4: 33-37). The Gospels recount five other instances connecting Jesus with exorcism, including a reference to Mariam from Magdala from whom seven demons had been cast out (Luke 8:2).

The exact nature of the afflictions, the instances, timing and locations of such cures, do not matter as much as that the Gospel authors clearly indicate that this is the kind of thing that Jesus became known for and an understanding amongst first-generation Christians that these cures included Gentiles. (For example, the 'long-distance' healing of the daughter of the distraught Syrophoenician mother.)

What does matter, also, is the faith of the one asking for healing and Jesus' authority in responding.

6.3a Possession

Few of us are not, one way or another, the dad, the mum, the aunt, the granddad, the brother or the child of someone possessed...

- *The Parent: fits that come out of the blue; just when we start to relax, an epileptic storm erupts over the golden curls; a monster in the dark taunts us, lying quiet and then springing out to shock us fresh each time. We live with fear – and the guilt of what we might have done, or not done. All the 'if only-s'.*
- *The Aunt: she is tied in chains by muscles and tendons that will not cooperate. Her spirit shines out at me. And this damnable inability to join with friends, to chat easily. We hear about a new approach, a possibility, someone who fixes this sort of thing. The news reviews are good. Something might come of this. I tend the withered aloe in our dried-out garden.*
- *The Grandparent: she is violent, angry, throwing furniture and abuse. She is trapped unable to get out... addiction binds her round, dragging on her as she takes each step forward. It creeps up on her in quiet moments, luring her to taste its release; promising freedom and taking it away in one second. Youth, years, relationships. Years on this journey back – if only it could be as instant as the Gospel says.*
- *The Colleague: the ASD, BPD, OCD, schizoid, bi-polar, manic depressed colleague and all the other initialled people we've pigeon-holed off as 'abnormal', not 'one of*

us', the constant slicing of the sausage until all we've got left is our selves made in our own image.
- The Brother: he rants and raves, is constantly compelled and cannot rest; a chronic fidget-er of the mind and body, driving his closest people away, exhausting himself on wild schemes.
- The Carer: what I had done to cause this situation? God knows, I'm plagued with guilt. Blame flows through the taps in our home; shame hangs at the windows.
- The Self: the swings and troughs and highs that toss me around; outbursts that cost friends and jobs and security. I am possessed by spirits I did not ask for and I cannot shake. Sometimes, I even want to be possessed with this manic energy, it energises me.

Then, someone comes who wants to release me. Someone cares enough to spend the time with me, to focus their attention upon me. Someone who can see in me, me, a promise, a bud, a seed, a young sapling. Someone looks closely enough; whose spirit enters mine. Someone who calms me by being present to the person who is me.

Someone wants to stay by me, ease the pressure; trickle life-saving-balm through my veins and my brain and my neurones and the muscles in my tongue and limbs and twitching eyes and face and head. Someone speaks authoritatively, bringing healing.

I am heartened. I know now it is possible. A helping hand steadies me. A calming hand soothes me. Teaching me words I haven't said before: I can believe.

6.3b A father's perspective

Nothing looks more full of sorrow[84]
than his mother's face when demon seizures
cast him on the ground and

boys who were his playmates
just one scuffle ago run screaming 'devilry'
into their mother's skirts;

or his puzzlement as he sits solitary
in the doorway not knowing why we closet him
away from taunts and stares;

or her silent sobs each time
I turn away from her at night, each of us gagging
on our private guilt and blame.

We hear there is a healer
who has come who's laid his hands on cripples
and left them whole.

I beg him, *Pity, Sir, some pity,
save us from the devil's strangling of our child.*
He talks to me about our son –

no-one ever has before –
wanting to know everything about our boy
and as he gazes at the little fellow,
nothing looks more like sorrow.

---

[84] Opening line taken with permission from Judith Beveridge, 'Fogbox, Scotland' in *New Poems*, Giramondo Press, Western Sydney University, 2018, page 211.

6.4 Touch

Reading

Mark 8:22-25

Place

This story is situated in the fishing village of Bethsaida on the northern end of Sea of Galilee, where Jesus spent a lot of time, now buried under the shores that have become silted up over the centuries.

At this site, it is easy to imagine a bustling port and administrative centre, the comings and goings of people around the paved roadways, the small stone homes where fishermen lived; where women went to the market and the well, busy about very ordinary chores, with the knowledge of each other's business that comes from living at close quarters.

Context

Mark's is the only account of this healing of a blind man at Bethsaida, but in the memory of the early followers, this is the sort of thing typical of Jesus' healing action during his ministry. In Mark 10:46-52, the Gospel author recounts the healing of Bartimaeus outside Jericho – a rare occasion when the cured person was named. Scholars suggest that this is because Bartimaeus (in Luke and Mark's versions) subsequently joined the group of those following Jesus. Other stories of the blind being healed occur in John chapter 9 and Matthew 11:5 (paralleled in Luke 7:22).

The healing at Bethsaida is situated in Mark's Gospel after the second of two feeding (Eucharistic) stories and Jesus' attempt to revise this lesson with his disciples – and get through to them. The healing is followed immediately by Peter's profession of faith with Mark implying that maybe, finally, Peter, at least, has 'got' what Jesus is on about.

I try to imagine I am the blind man.

6.4a Seeing

my eyes
bear scales of shame
and yet
I do not understand
what I have done

A shadow falls upon me. Someone so close I feel his breath. *What do you want?* 'What do *you* want?' he asks. *If only I could see.* He takes my hand and guides me till the market noises fade. I'm not afraid: I've long since learned the difference between men, and this man means no harm.

I feel
warm pressure
on my eyes
after all these years
someone's touching me

'Go home', he says. I open up my eyes. The brightness hurts.

6.4b Being Infected

Reading

Leviticus 13:45-46, 14:1-32
Single leper healed: Mark 1:40-45, Matthew 8:1-4, Luke 5:12-16
Healing of ten lepers: Luke 17:11-19
Naaman the Aramean is cleansed of leprosy through the prophet Elisha: 2 Kings 5

Place

Probably not relevant but somewhere in Galilee. The healing of the single leper was probably around Capernaum.

Context

Healing lepers was something associated with Jesus. In the thinking of the time, sickness was not just a physical affliction. In the words of Juan Pagola, *as the Israelites saw it, a strong and vigorous life is a life blessed by God; a sick, wounded or mutilated life is a curse.*[85]

---

[85] Pagola, page 159.

'Leprosy' as mentioned in the Gospels probably referred to a whole range of skin diseases. (The *Jerusalem Bible* calls it 'a virulent skin disease'.) The result was the same: isolation and shame for those afflicted with these disfiguring ailments. They were regarded as unclean and separated from the community. They might well have thought God had abandoned them.[86]

The word Mark uses to describe Jesus' reaction can mean pity or compassion or indignation. With the allusions to Hebrew prophets (2 Kings 5), the Gospel of Mark is claiming Jesus is a prophet of the kingdom of God.

Luke's account of the healing of ten lepers (17:11-19) includes the return of one – a Samaritan – who offered thanks. This story in Luke is placed after a series of teachings and before more teachings warning about false prophets. This prophet, Jesus, not only heals the leper, but a leper who is a foreigner.

6.4c A prophet who embraces

a leper
chained in misery
unlocks
God-like compassion
from a stranger

he stretches
out his hand
to touch
all that is blighted
he restores in me

---

[86] Myrick C. Shinall jr, 'The Social Condition of Lepers in the Gospels' in *Journal of Biblical Literature*, Volume 137, No 4, Winter 2018, pages 915-934, http://dx.doi.org/10.15699/jbl.1372.2018.454556

6.4d Feeling untouchable

It's not just Covid that can isolate us, set us apart. It can also come through:

- failure – in career, a job, a relationship
- not fitting within the social norms of acceptability
- being poor in an affluent society
- lacking power in a self-sufficient culture
- being 'other' in race, gender, culture...
- mental illness, addiction and other conditions
- being outspoken once too often
- rejecting prevailing assumptions.

6.4e Infection and isolation

I live
apart in isolation
stained with shame
even my old neighbours
rush past, faces in their hands

he's here:
the one they say who heals –
dare I risk
one more humiliation –
I have nothing more to lose

in my stinking rags
I edge towards him
surely, he sees me
for what I am –
he does not flinch

        emboldened,
       I throw myself
        into the dust,
          beg him
       to make me clean

        he reaches down
       pulls me to my feet,
         embraces me –
        I try to pull away,
        he holds me still

       you are clean he says
        his hand still on me
        I raise my head –
       when was the last time
      I gazed in someone's face?

       go, tell the priests,
      show them you are clean
            he says
     give them their offerings –
     you owe them nothing more

        and tell no-one.
        I see myself afresh
         and I am clean –
          how can I not
          tell everyone?

          I watch him
          walk alone
         away from town
        his cloak pulled up
      to mask his head and face

Jesus' actions cost him. He responded from his gut, the Gospels say. He followed his heart. He reached out to society's untouchables and acted. He seemed unconcerned that he might become infected. When the word spread (as it had to), Jesus left the built-up colonies where people lived. 'Led by the Spirit' to respond to the leper, he chose to seek the desert.

6.5 His mother's only son

Reading

Son of a widow of Nain: Luke 7:11-17, 1 Kings 17:17-24
Regarding widows in Hebrew scriptures: Deuteronomy 26:12, Exodus 22:21-23, Isaiah 1:17, Jeremiah 7:5-6

Place

Nain was, and is, a small settlement about 14 kilometres south of Nazareth situated on slopes that look towards Mount Tabor. In the 1st century CE, Nain is thought to have had only a small number of families and was relatively poor.

Context

Nain was 'off the beaten track' and the *New International Version* translation of Luke's – the only account – of this story describes it as taking place *soon after* the healing of the Centurion's servant in Capernaum, about 40 kilometres away, moving from 180 metres below sea level to Nain (about 200 metres above sea level).

Luke situates the story in the period before the murder of the Baptiser, as part of the answer to John who had sent messengers to Jesus asking, 'Are you the one who is to come?' By this time, we read, Jesus' reputation is spreading through the region.

Another memory of Jesus raising the dead to life is recorded in the Gospel story of the little girl, the daughter of Jairus. That story is told in detail in Mark 5, Matthew 9 and Luke 8.

Perhaps Jesus was particularly responsive to children and their anguished parents.

6.5a Something happened at Nain that day

Such a small out-of-the-way place it was. Having risen early, we'd been climbing most of the day. Quite a crowd with us, more than our usual band. People joining in as we passed by, curious, I suppose. And Jesus so determined to reach there – somewhere – moving us along.

We came up the slope towards the hamlet. There was jostling. Yahooing. Some young ones raced towards the gate, the slower ones egging them on. High spirits as they sensed the slogging walk was almost done; we women following towards the rear, glad too.

And then, confusion. A crowd coming from the town tangled with ours as we were entering. We knew at once from the mournful dirge of flutes that someone had died. Wailing, as they threw dust in their hair and down their clothes, women led a procession towards the burial site. Our group fell silent and we paused so they could pass with their sobbing and keening and piercing music.

'A young man', the word passed from mouth to mouth, people on tiptoe to see, 'an only son, and his dad already dead'. I saw Jesus looking for someone in the crowd among the women. Then, a local pointed out to him one woman amongst the others – a face like wax, distraught, limp. 'That's her, see, poor thing. A widow. And now her son too.'

Jesus moved until he stood before her. He put one hand gently on her shoulder and spoke to her. She paused, startled for a moment. Then she looked up and his face was so tender-sad. 'Don't cry', he said, 'please don't be so sad'. And all the time, he too was weeping.

Then he walked towards the bier that followed her. The poor lad, even in all his funeral cloths, made such a small mound upon the board. Did Jesus think before he put out his hand to touch the litter the corpse was laid on? He stood right there, held it, so the bearers had to stop.

By now, the flutes had ceased and even the women ceased their noise as people watched the interruption. And in the silence, Jesus' voice came through – quietly, firmly – 'Get up, young man. Get up. Your mother needs you'. A shock rippled through the crowd. Unease. Uncertainty.

Then a shout: 'He's moving. He's alive'. The men carrying the bier almost dropped it on the ground. Hesitating, at first, they began to unravel the binding cloths, while we were all agog not believing what we were seeing. The young man sat up. He looked around at all the faces staring at him. 'What's happening?'

Jesus simply looked to his mother and beckoned her to come close. She clasped her son – he was, after all, a mere lad of about 14 – weeping, touching his face, staring into his eyes and then carefully she untied the cloths around his feet so he could stand. 'Here is your son,' Jesus said to her. 'Take him home'. The other women came around to lead them both away.

People were stunned of course. 'Who is this man?' they asked each other as they dispersed. 'Is this Elijah?' they wondered together in awe. 'Is this Elisha the prophet come back again?'

Looking back, I remember the wonder, the sense that God had sent a new prophet to his people. Mostly I remember the look on Jesus' face, how he felt for that poor mother in her distress.

Something happened at Nain that day.

6.5b The widow's story

this morning
I was nothing –
no longer wife
no longer mother
belonging no-where

only family
touch the dead
without defilement
today the Nazarene
became my family

I sit here
through the evening
with my son
restored...
wondering

6.6 Time to think differently

> a blind man cured
> a deaf mute healed
> bread in abundance
> help on troubled waters:
> time to think differently

Something to think about

'A "miracle" can be defined as an event which produces wonder and acts as a sign of the presence and actions of God. It is sometimes assumed that for an event to be a miracle, it must be outside the laws of nature and beyond any possible scientific explanation. This is completely beside the point. For a miracle it is required that the event be such as to produce amazement or wonder in those witnessing it. A cure, for example, may be explicable in terms of psychotherapy, and yet still be a miracle.'[87]

*

Generally, the ancient Greco-Roman world accepted miracles 'as part of the religious landscape' and included a messy mixture of the miraculous and the magical. The Gospel miracles were performed with the overriding purpose of being signs and realisations of the gracious power of the God of Israel acting through Jesus.[88] John Meier concludes that healing, casting out demons, raising the dead were the sort of thing that Jesus did and 'any historian... not giving

---

[87] Fallon, page 146.
[88] This section has been summarised from John Meier, *Mentor, Message and Miracles*, Vol II *A Marginal Jew, Rethinking the Historical Jesus*, New York, Doubleday, 1994. pages 512, 535-545.

weight to Jesus' fame as a miracle worker is not delineating this strange and complex Jew'.[89]

*

Just as God... 'rescued the Chosen People in the Psalms, hushing the storm to a gentle breeze, stilling the billows of the sea, bringing them to their desired haven, so too Jesus rescues the disciples; so too he rescues us'. The scripture scholars John Donohue and Daniel Harrington tell us: 'Jesus possesses the same power over the forces of chaos that characterizes the Lord of hosts. Mark's readers would be led to see that Jesus is the agent of God's power who ultimately triumphs over the forces that threaten the community with extinction'.

'No doubt we think we have our share of upsets and disturbances to confront in church, society and the world. Mark was writing for a community who experienced the full catastrophe. They "had experienced the upsurge of the power of chaos and evil during Nero's persecution and the civil turmoil in Rome following his death in 68 and during (or shortly before) the Jewish War of 66–73 CE". Mark's first readers and listeners were like the disciples, crying out "Teacher, do you not care that we are perishing?" We, like them, are invited to continue the journey toward a deeper and more profound faith in the midst of chaos.'[90]

---

[89] Meier, Vol II, page 970.
[90] Frank Brennan SJ 'Father Frank's Homily 20th June 2021', *Catholic Outlook*, https://catholicoutlook.org/fr-franks-homily-20-june-2021/. Quotes are from John Donahue and Daniel Harrington, *The Gospel of Mark*, The Liturgical Press, Collegeville, 2002, pages 161, 162.

7

Breath of Wisdom

Mosaic, Church of the Transfiguration, Mount Tabor

7.1 Sophia, the Wisdom of God

Reading

Wisdom is of God: Job 28, Sirach: 24:3-7
Present in creation: Proverbs 8:22-31
Wisdom begins with 'fear of the Lord': Proverbs 1:7, 15:33, 31:30, Psalm 111:10
Delights of Wisdom: Wisdom 6:12-21, 7:7-14, 7:22 to 8:1
A saviour to the Hebrew people: Wisdom 10:15-18
Sophia, Wisdom woman: Sirach (Ecclesiasticus) 4:11, 24:1

Context

The understanding of *Wisdom* as an element of the divine is present in the later Hebrew scriptures, especially the Books of Wisdom. *Wisdom* is associated with 'fear of the Lord', which has been described less as 'fear' per se, but more a life lived in loving devotion and close relationship with the Sacred. Such mindfulness of the Holy leaves us with a sense of awe, a sense of our own miniscule place in the order of things. In the words of Kathleen O'Connor, 'only those who have entered this relationship can recognise the wisdom and harmony pulsing through the universe'.[91]

Wisdom in the Hebrew scriptures is portrayed as feminine. She is personified as 'Sophia'. She was present at creation and in creation. She is easy to find for those who seek.

7.1a Sophia, the Wisdom of God

I.
in the beginning
before the world was shaped
before mountains grew
before springs began to flow
across fields and dust

I was there,
in a mist upon the earth
and a cloud above
aurora lights in the north
a comet diving south

---

[91] Quoted in Denis Edwards, *Jesus the wisdom of God*, Homebush: St Pauls, 1995, page 49.

I was there,
constantly at his side,
filled with delight
in all human beings,
at play with the Creator[92]

II.
his people
fled their oppressors
by night
I was all starry light
a flare above deep waters[93]

III.
I am a mirror
reflecting God's goodness
making all things new,
subtle, pervasive, quick:
I am the breath of God[94]

7.1b Jesus: Wisdom of God

Reading

Matthew 11:25-30, John 1:1-18, 6:35
1 Corinthians 1: 22-31, Philippians 2:6-11, Colossians 1:15-20,
2:2-3, Hebrews 1:3
Wisdom 7:21-27, Proverbs 8:22, 9:1-6

---

[92] cf. Proverbs 8:22-31, Sirach /Ecclesiasticus 24:3-5.
[93] cf. Wisdom 10:15-18.
[94] cf. Wisdom 7:22-8:1.

Context

It seems that the Christian communities very early on identified Jesus with Sophia, the Wisdom of God. John's Gospel opens with a Prologue that reads like a poem. The association of Jesus with divine Wisdom appears later in John 6:35 which overlaps strongly with Proverbs 9:1-6.

Apart from early hymns (e.g. Philippians 2:6-11), there are references to Jesus in the Letters of Paul (e.g. Colossians and 1 Corinthians) that link him directly with Wisdom. Jewish disciples hearing the Letter to the Hebrews would immediately recognise the direct reference to divine Wisdom found in Wisdom 7:26.

Different translations of the text in Hebrews enhance the insight about Jesus that the early Christian community had developed. Jesus is variously described in Hebrews 1:3 as being 'the reflection of God's glory and the perfect expression of his very being' (*New Catholic Bible*) or 'the reflection of God's glory and bears the *impress* of God's own being' (*New Jerusalem Bible*).

This early Christian insight highlights a God who is neither male nor female and links the man Jesus with the divine feminine Wisdom Sophia.

7.1c Wisdom's compassion

Reading

Proverbs 1, Proverbs 2, Luke 6:36, Matthew 5:7, 1 John 4:7-8

Response

The idea of 'God' is central to trying to understand something of the person of Jesus. Yet it is a challenging concept for many of us. One insight coming through the lens of Wisdom is that 'God' remains incomprehensible to us: always more expansive than we can imagine, always more merciful, always more inclusive, always more compassionate. Jesus came as teacher of God's kingdom; he shone God's Wisdom upon the situations of those who were poor, marginalised or broken in any way, and it revealed a God of uncompromising compassion.

Jesus was seen in the early Church, not only as teaching about the Wisdom of God but was himself seen as the divine Wisdom enfleshed. 'Jesus is so Spirit-led, so caught up in love with the God of boundless compassion, and so lives this compassion in liberating action, inclusive community and familial relationships', writes Denis Edwards, 'that it becomes clear, in the light of resurrection, that Jesus is divine Wisdom among us'.[95]

soft, red
wax stamped
with an impression –
infinite compassion,
the face of God

---

[95] Denis Edwards, page 50.

7.2 Finding Wisdom

Reading

Syrophoenician woman: Mark 7:24-30, Matthew 15:21-28
Samaritan woman: John 4:1-42
Widow: Luke 7:11-17
Peter's mother-in-law: Matthew 8:14-15, Mark 1:29-31, Luke 4:38-39
Woman in Simon's house: Matthew 26:6-13, Mark 14:3-9, Luke 7:36-50
Bent woman: Luke 13:10-17
Adulterous woman: John 7:53 to 8:11
Family of Jesus: Matthew 12:46-50, Mark 3:31-35, Luke 8:19-21, 11:27-28

Context

The Gospels reflect Jesus as someone who noticed women, who was not deterred by their status and responded to their immediate grounded situations. We read of him attending to the hurt and illnesses of women, regardless of whether they were children, widows, Gentiles (Samaritan and Syrophoenician), ritually unclean or regarded as sinners. In addition, he included in his close band of followers women whom he had healed, such as Mariam of Magdala and Joanna. The loving compassion of God moved him.

7.2a Healing of two women

Reading

Jairus' daughter: Matthew 9:18-19, 23-26, Mark 5:21-24a, 35-43, Luke 8:40-42, 49-56
Haemorrhaging woman: Matthew 9:20-22, Mark 5:24b-34, Luke 8:43-48

Context

There was a young girl of twelve and a woman who had suffered for twelve years. In all three Synoptics, the story of the haemorrhaging woman is spliced between the two parts of the story about the young girl. Why?

Both stories are rich in detail and dialogue, and wonderfully human. Mark's version is the longest and includes the detail that the older woman had 'endured much' under many doctors and that her condition was worsening. Why such detailed attention by the evangelists to these two stories of healing?

The version in chapter 5 in Mark, like Luke's, is preceded by the account of Jesus healing a demented man living in a graveyard 'on the other side' of the Sea in the Gentile land of the Gerasenes. Like the story of the healing of the young and the older woman, the healing of the madman is told in fascinating detail; the healed man goes on to spread news of Jesus in the Greek area nearby.

Response

If you are a mum or dad who has a child with fever or a serious illness,
if you are desperately begging for healing for a child or loved one,
if you scour the internet looking to understand their situation,
if your panic threatens to swamp your belief in possibilities,
if you sometimes feel your child's situation is hopeless,
if people ridicule you for seeing small improvements,
if you are a child and feel alone and frightened,
if you are a young girl at the point of puberty,
if you can put your faith in people of goodness,
... then take comfort in the story of Jairus' daughter and Jesus' healing touch.

If you have endured long years of illness,
if you are regularly afflicted with heavy blood flows,
if you experience isolation because of your condition,
if you spend day after day in medical consultations and waiting rooms,
if you have endured the discomfort and embarrassment of invasive treatments,
if the medical costs not covered by insurance and the Government leave you impoverished,
if you feel humiliated to speak of your condition and your actions,
if you resist the press of every obstacle in your search for wellness,
if you reach out with your own power to grasp healing,
if you know your body so well you know when you are healed,
if you continue to hope for better things,
if you can put your faith in goodness,
... then take comfort in the story of the bleeding woman who dared to reach out and take Jesus' healing power to herself.

7.2b Unlikely models of Wisdom

Reading

Lost coin: Luke 15:8-10
Persistent widow: Luke 18:1-18
Widow of Zarephath: Luke 4:24-26
Wise virgins: Matthew 25:1-13
Widow's mite: Mark 2:41-44, Luke 21:1-4
Teaching against divorce and lust: Matthew 5:27-29, 31-33

Context

At times in the Gospels, Jesus cites unexpected models for his teaching about God's kingdom. Not only did he show compassion to women, he also quoted women as models of faith.

In the story of the lost coin, a woman is the central character who seeks what she has lost and then celebrates its discovery.

In the story of the widow who wanted justice, it is the widow's threatening persistence and the judge's fear of her hassling him that wins out. Neither character is attractive: the judge is unjust, irreligious and reluctant to help, only doing so from self-interest; the widow is shrill, wanting vengeance against her opponents. We don't know from the story that her case is justified, only that she is persistent.

In Jesus' address in the synagogue at Nazareth, his listeners were provoked by his reference to Elijah because he claimed Elijah was responding, not to widows in Israel, but to a widow at Zarephath: not only a woman, but a widow who was a Gentile. Further, some women such as the Syrophoenician woman and the woman suffering from a haemorrhage, called forth his power from him.

Response

You shocked me with your response to your mother when she came looking for you. 'Your mother and brothers are here', they said. And you replied, pointing to your disciples, not your family, 'Here are my mother and brothers'. It seems a pretty hurtful thing for a mum to hear.

Yet, in other ways, you showed that you had heeded the women in your life and had learnt to be sensitive to them. You noticed widows and responded to them with kindness. You showed an understanding of how women were disadvantaged by men's power to divorce them. You used the lives and circumstances of women to shape your stories and teaching.

I'd like to think you consulted with some of the women before you told that story about the yeast. Or the lost coin. Or of the feisty widow. Did you ask for feedback from Mariam, Joanna and the other women in your band about how the story had gone over the first few times? And did you learn from them and modify it a little?

Perhaps the truth you wanted to teach over and over, even to your own mum, was that nothing was more important than doing the will of God. Since she and Joseph had nurtured you into your faith, she may not have been surprised. You also said that when any of us does put God first and central in our lives, we are as close to you as your own mother, your sister or your brother. That's pretty amazing.

7.2c Children as models of Wisdom

Reading

Let the children come: Matthew 19:13-15, Mark 10:13-16, Luke 18:15-17
Wisdom revealed: Matthew 11:25-27, Luke 10:21-24

Context

Jesus began his public life calling people to repent because the kingdom of heaven was near: to have a change of heart, to turn around and see things from a different perspective. This perspective is the lens of the Wisdom of God. One sharp turn-around in thinking is to see Wisdom revealed through children.

Children

Some decades ago, extensions and renovations to our local railway station were opened by the Prime Minister. His name was well known in the household as my husband and I actively supported his policies and political party. We went along with our children to the ceremonies on the Saturday morning of the opening. Towards the end of the formalities, our daughter, who was then about six, sidled up to the great man and took his hand in her soft little one – as she would for an uncle or family friend.

What was his response? Nothing. He neither disengaged his hand, nor squeezed hers back, nor bent down to see who had taken this bold step, nor spoke a word to her. He simply ignored her soft little fingers. This, she told us there and then, was what disappointed her. Even a courteous reprimand would have satisfied her more.

We could find some good reasons for the Prime Minister to ignore this approach by a child (perhaps). These days, of course, she would not have been able to get so close: Federal Police would have the PM cordoned off, thereby preventing any such embarrassments.

In Matthew 19:13-15, some parents were bringing their small children for Jesus to touch and bless. Like the fiercest security detail, the disciples in all three accounts 'sternly ordered' the mums and dads to take their kids away.

Unlike the Prime Minister who simply ignored our small daughter's spontaneous and trusting touch, Jesus responded strongly. He was 'indignant', according to Mark's Gospel. 'Indignant' is an unusually strong word, rarely used in the Gospels in relation to Jesus. Which makes me wonder: just how polite or gentle were those gatekeeping disciple-minders? After all, there were no media cameras to record them.

'Let them come to me', he berated his disciples. 'What makes you think you can stop them? I love these little kids. My Dad's kingdom belongs to such as these children.'

It's a sobering thought if you are in a position of some authority, that sometimes we might be unaware that people around us are sternly keeping others (especially 'little people') away.

7.2d Being like children

Reading

Proverbs 8:30-31, Matthew 19:13-15

Wisdom is revealed to the simple: my world, says Jesus, is for people who are like little kids.

If I were like a little child, I might:
- tramp dirt across the kitchen floor
- climb all over whoever visits the house
- study ants instead of coming in for dinner
- forget to wash my hands
- wear my rain boots on the wrong feet
- ask my aunty why her nose is so big (or red)...

and, if so, this might be because:
- play is my work, and work my play
- every person is my important friend
- I find wonder in the infinitesimal
- I earnestly believe in what you tell me
- the familiarities of each day continually surprise me, and
- my every moment contains eternity.

If you wish to enter God's kingdom, see and grasp it as a small child would.

7.3 Wisdom from the kitchen

Reading

Matthew 13:33, Luke 13:20-21

Context

This very short story is set in Matthew's Gospel amidst a number of 'the kingdom is like' stories.

It is easy to domesticate the parables. It is too easy to allegorise them, taking each element and finding a moralistic parallel. The result is a disappointing banality. This reduces the shock that the parables would have had for Jesus' listeners; and, of course, reduces their impact on us. To take the parables and apply them in a formulaic way is to reduce their power. Our challenge as readers is to try to hear them, to let the images speak and not turn them into moral fables

So it was important for me to learn that three measures (sixty pounds) of flour in the first century CE approximates 18-27 kilograms of flour. We're talking excess here, enough to make 36-54 one-kilogram loaves of bread. And the yeast used is likely to be more akin to sour-dough starter than granules of yeast.

7.3a The big bake-off

Did you hear the one about the woman who put sour dough starter into 27 kilos of flour? All that yeast and all that flour!

She must have gone crazy. Everyone knows that once the yeast is in the flour, there's no stopping the fermentation. You can't ferment so much and then just put it all aside. Sure, you can reserve a small amount, but once you mix the dough, you need to bake: all 27 kilos of it.

She would have blown the family budget with one action.

Can you imagine the tantalising sour smell throughout the house and village? Everyone would have known she was setting dough. Where did she put it? As it rose and rose and rose. No-one has pans enough for 40-50 loaves of bread.

Unless she's going commercial. And I don't think Jesus was arguing for a kingdom that was mechanised and made for profit.

There would have been dough everywhere. And baking it! Too much for home. The village bakery would have been running hot all day and night to get the loaves produced before it went too sour and was ruined. And then, enough loaves, not just for family and neighbours and friends, but for strangers, enemies, transients, in fact, anyone who might have happened to be in that woman's village that day.

I imagine that people in the village are still talking about that bake-off. That was something to remember:

- the extravagance of it
- the generosity of it
- the recklessness of it
- the unquestioning inclusiveness of it
- the all or nothing decisiveness of her action
- the holding-nothing-back determination when she poured all that yeast mix into the bins of flour.

Now, why would Jesus use this as an image of the kingdom?

7.3b An idli bonanza

Had he lived in South India or Sri Lanka, Jesus might have told his story using a woman making idlis. Idlis are a delicacy made from steaming cakes of fomented rice and lentils. After grinding, the rice and lentils are left to foment. The batter rises and expands in the warm air, doubling in volume.

In the instance of the story in Matthew 13:33, the woman would have made enough batter to fill two bathtubs (or more) and to make over 600 idlis.

Who might we invite to share in such a breakfast banquet? Surely not just our immediate friends and close ones. Idlis are best eaten fresh from the steamer: we would need to break through our normal polite reticence about those whom we invite home and those whom we don't. We would need to beg people to come and share in the feast.

Such is the transformational extravagance of God's love. It is for everyone.

7.3c Finding the Wisdom of God in the domestic

I like the fact that in the story of the yeast, Jesus chose to make a woman his protagonist and that she found Wisdom in her kitchen.

Other stories, like the one of the missing money, also have domestic settings. The woman turns on all the lights (or lamps) and turns the house upside down, searching for what she has lost. I find a thorough spring clean of my life from time to time is always useful in re-orienting me to what is important; in rediscovering my focus, in recentering. And yes, I do want to dance and celebrate when I turn again to the mystery of God's presence.

Some of this mystery is beautifully suggested in Seamus Heaney's poem, 'Sunlight', one of two poems written, I understand, for his mother. The poet moves gently into the kitchen, describing a woman kneading bread on a hot afternoon with 'whitened nails' and 'floury apron', sharing lovingly, as wholeheartedly as the woman in Matthew 13:33.[96] The unseen presence of those for whom the woman bakes the bread run through the poem. It is love in action.

The domesticity of these parables tells us, as Amy-Jill Levine writes, that 'despite all our images of golden slippers and harps and halos, the kingdom is present at the communal oven of a Galilean village where everyone has enough to eat'. She suggests that the parables describe the kingdom that works its way through all aspect of our lives and 'is present, inchoate, in everything'.[97]

7.4 Unexpected Wisdom

There are many parables about the kingdom of God (or the kingdom of heaven in Matthew) in the Gospels. The challenge for us as contemporary readers is to move beyond their familiarity to try to hear them as Jesus' contemporaries might have heard them. Our challenge is that there is little unexpected in the parables – after all, we know the endings, don't we? On the other hand, for Jesus' listeners there were elements of the unexpected. How we learn from them today can be enriched by how we understand their 1st CE Jewish context.

I have selected only a few.

---

[96] Seamus Heaney, 'Sunlight' in 'Mossbawn: Two Poems in Dedication' for Mary Heaney, 1975 https://www.nobelprize.org/prizes/literature/1995/8422-poetry/

[97] Levine, chapter 3, page 137.

7.4a The bags of gold

Reading

Matthew 25:14-30, Luke 19:11-27, Matthew 25:31-46

Context

Whoever the actual evangelist might have been, it is generally believed Matthew's Gospel was written sometime after the destruction of Jerusalem and the temple by the Romans in 70CE. Writing from within and for his community, Matthew would have been influenced by the community's historical context in shaping his Gospel.

The parable of the talents (pounds) in Matthew follows chapter 24 which focuses on 'end times' false prophets and the coming of the Son of Man unexpectedly. The chapter opens with Jesus' prediction of the destruction of the temple. With the temple so important in Jewish life and the physical structure still in the process of its massive extension by Herod, these words shocked and angered many. Chapter 24 concludes with a parable contrasting two slaves – one who is faithful, wise and ready for his master's return and the other, who takes advantage of his master's absence and who will be punished.

In chapter 25, the parable of the talents (or pounds) is placed between a story about ten marriage attendants and one about the last judgment. These three parables also include the theme of readiness for the coming of the kingdom begun in chapter 24; all three highlight the contrast between those who are ready and those who are not: wise versus foolish bridesmaids, trustworthy versus worthless workers, and compassionate 'sheep' versus callous 'goats'. The parable of the last judgment sums up in familiar words what is required of us as we await the kingdom. 'For I was hungry...'

Chapter 26 takes us straight into the Passion narrative.

7.4a Reading the story (I)

The use of the word 'talents' to identify the parable in Matthew 25:14-30 can be misleading because it is too readily associated with the meaning of 'abilities'. Rather, in 1st CE, a talent was a monetary measure, in fact the highest unit of currency in the Greek world. In Jesus' time, it was worth about 6000 denarii, that is, equivalent to a labourer's wages for about 6000 days, or about 20 years' of labour. In short, the man going abroad possessed incredible wealth, a wildly extravagant wealth, which evokes immediate interest. It's a 'once upon a time' kind of story designed to engage listeners.

How would Jesus' listeners have heard the story? What would they have heard? The man left his managers with colossal wealth with the expectation of them making more wealth. They would be expected to do so in the way the man himself did – through exploitation of peasant farmers. The wealthy man says of himself that he reaped where he did not sow and gathered where he did not scatter. Jesus' listeners would have known from their lived experience how the stewards made their profits. In a bad year, farmers would need to borrow from the rich, with only their land as collateral; when the farmers were unable to repay the loan, the wealthy landowners appropriated their land, reducing them to being tenants or day labourers. I have seen parallels in India. This sort of activity flourishes still today, especially in largely (but not only) agrarian societies.

The man gave to each of his stewards according to their status in his household. The two more senior ones measured up to his expectation: doubling the money for him. They didn't question his approach – and in fact had vested interest in pursuing his approach to earn their own cut on the side.

7.4a Reading the story (II)

For curiosity's sake, and to help us gauge the impact of the parable, a comparison with current Australian figures can be hypothesised. If the lowest average salary in Australia in 2020 was around $23,700, one talent would be worth conservatively around $500,000, two talents about $1 million and five talents about $2.5 million.[98]

And so, in contemporary terms, the story could be about a property developer who goes overseas and gives his newest recruit half a million to be responsible for during his absence. He gives his Department Head $1 million. He gives his Deputy $2.5 million. 'Look after it for me', he says to each of them. He's made his fortune in real estate, insider trading on the stock market, alliances with corrupt politicians and exploitative miners. He is tough on his tenants. He pays next to no tax. Buys land up cheap (for airports) and sells it dear. Builds cheap apartments. He comes back. The young recruit has done nothing. He can't bring himself to continue in the same way as his employer.

In the Gospel story, the least able steward knew what was expected but he didn't act on it. Was he lazy? Was he

---

[98] The minimum award wage in Australia in 2021 is quoted at $40,000 but I have stayed with the lower figure.

frightened of the master? Or was he showing moral courage? Was he trying to break the cycle of the master's oppression and exploitation? He buried it. He kept it safe. He didn't steal it from the master. But nor did he exploit other people.

And his reward? He was thrown out. He lost his job. No doubt, his name as a steward was ruined. But maybe he could now live with himself – and more importantly, perhaps, he could live with his neighbours and the community... is this what Jesus meant? Maybe he was freed from his slavery... in the sense of freeing himself from compulsion to keep on exploiting.

Perhaps Jesus is saying that the kingdom is unpopular with the powerful. Maybe he is saying the kingdom is not found in exploiting people and concentrating on wealth creation. Maybe he is saying the kingdom might land you in trouble.

An alternative reading comes when we see Jesus as a prophet to Israel, highlighted by Matthew's location of the parable. Was he saying that the kingdom demands that we put aside fear and take risks and invest wherever we can? John Meier suggests reading the parable as an 'exhortation-plus-warning spoken by Jesus to his disciples to rise to the challenge of his demanding call to leave all and follow him... Jesus is insistent: along with sovereign grace, serious demand, and superabundant reward comes the possibility of being condemned for refusing the demand contained in the gift'. But then, Jesus might also have been addressing the whole of Israel to realise its vocation as the chosen People.[99]

Immediately after the parable of the talents, Matthew portrays Jesus describing the Last Judgment. Here, the

---

[99] Meier, Volume V, pages 306-310.

message is clear and unambiguous: 'Just as you offered mercy and compassion to the least members of my family, then you offered it to me'.

7.4b Seeds and other buried things

Reading

Seed growing secretly: Mark 4:26-29
Mustard seed: Matthew 13:31-32, Mark 4:30-32, Luke 13:18-19
A farmer sows seed: Matthew 13:1-9, Mark 4:3-9, Luke 8:5-8
Weeds among wheat: Matthew 13:36-43
A valuable pearl: Matthew 13:45-46
Net filled with fish: Matthew 13:47-53
Hidden treasure: Matthew 13:44
Yeast: Matthew 13:33
Weeds and wheat: Matthew 13:24-30

Context

The stories about seeds, weeds, yeast and hidden treasure are set amongst other stories we know as parables. The stories of seeds and weeds offer some basic gardening advice, but of course, that is not why they are included in the Gospels. They are pithy stories, with those about hidden treasure and fabulous pearls having extra appeal. In

Matthew's Gospel, seven of the above parables are brought together in chapter 13. The chapter concludes with Jesus being rejected by his own townspeople (an incident which Mark and Luke locate in different circumstances).

Only Mark has the story of the seed growing secretly.

The parable of the Mustard Seed has been seen as pointing to the small, unimpressive beginnings of the kingdom in Jesus' ministry. For those who can see, the small and powerless, the kingdom is already present in Jesus' teaching and healing, giving promise of its fullness when the realm of God is fully in place. 'The contrast between beginning and end almost defies belief, but the grand climax of the kingdom is already present and guaranteed in its small beginnings.'[100]

Response

> yeast foments
> within the dough
> in its own time
> its work is done –
> I make a cup of tea... wait

We have planted carrot seeds. Now, long before they are ready, my daughter wants to pull up one of the plants to see if anything is forming. 'Not yet,' I counsel. 'Let it be.' Of course, she pulls it up while it is still growing and sees for herself what I was trying to say. 'Living things will grow but not if we mess with them.'

> in my garden
> an unruly flourish
> of weeds –
> the desire to control
> and have things ordered

---

[100] Meier, Volume V, page 373.

small shoots appear
beneath our curry leaf tree
each autumn
they do not ask to come
nor wait for me to call them

deep in the soil
drawing moisture
within, without
our interference
carrots will form

wheat grows
despite the weeds,
bread is made
warming our hearths
filling our hearts

like wild weeds
the kingdom grows
its coming
not of my design
or cultivation

it's not
just mustard seeds
something bigger
than us is happening–
I will learn to love the weeds

7.4c Day Labourers

Reading

Matthew 20:1-16

Context

According to Amy-Jill Levine, Jesus told his parable stories because they serve '... as keys that can unlock the mysteries we face by helping us ask the right questions. Jesus knew that the best teaching about how to live, and to live abundantly... comes from narratives that remind us of what we already know but are resistant to recall'. If we take them seriously as invitations and not as answers, the parables 'can continue to inform our lives, even as our lives continue to open up the parables to new readings'.[101]

Response

You stand there early, at the corner of our street in Chennai, near the roadside temple shrine where men in fresh-pressed white shirts offer morning puja, and diesel-smelling school vans collect fresh-pampered students. You're waiting in your bedraggled sari to be hired for some hours, or the day, if you're lucky, from among the twenty other men and women shuffling bare feet on the dusty tar in the bazaar. All of you faithful to the hope of getting, at least, something.

> burning leaves
> lifting sand and bricks
> sweeping the street...
> the certainty
> of nothing certain

---

[101] Levine, page 297.

They stand there early, at the corner near Hebron Road in Jerusalem, just near the exit out of Checkpoint 300. Already, coming through the checkpoint, they have crossed through misery. They wait, these men from Bethlehem, with their hope of daily work for vans to pick them up and take them to their sustenance in some dusty workplace, somewhere across the city.

> day labourers
> jostling to be the one
> the agent calls
> for some piece work,
> today's survival

In Western Sydney, a young school-early-leaver, unsupported and out-of-home, seeks work: 'Agency' jobs, one day at a time – clearing rubbish, promoting World Vision to commuters on their smart phones in the CBD, Central station, Coogee beach, here and there. No certainty of tomorrow's work. Enough pay just for today.

> he spends his pay
> on pizza and a joint
> smoking
> into a night as hazy
> as his future

7.5 Lessons for leaders

Reading

Who is the greatest: Matthew 18:1-5, Luke 9:46-48, Mark 9:33-37
An ambitious mother: Matthew 20:20-28, Mark 10:35-45

Context

Jesus must have told them this so many times. Here they are, facing the threats of what lies ahead, and the disciples are still arguing about who's the best. It just goes to show that his message was then, and is still now, countercultural. At heart, it is as simple as a child; in practice, in our personal lives and in our religious institutions, the message keeps getting corroded.

For Jesus, domination of others and making one's authority felt 'are wholly inappropriate in Christian leaders. All desire for precedence and privilege is to be excluded, the only greatness the disciples of Jesus should aspire to is that of service to others'.[102]

---

[102] Denis McBride, CSsR, *The Parables of Jesus*, Redemptorist Publications, Chawton, 1999, page 42.

7.5a Leadership 101

(Re-imagined from Mark 9:33-37 and 10:35-45)

This time, we came back home by quiet paths. He seemed to be deliberately avoiding other people as though he wanted time just with us. He spoke to us as we walked, and there was a sense of urgency in him, as though he sensed he was running out of time.

As usual, when we arrived at the house, the children ran out to meet us. After he'd greeted the family, he came back out to where the men were hanging around in the courtyard and where we women were sorting out our bundles. He called to us. We stopped our sorting of cloths and pots and sat down to listen just where we were. The men shuffled over to where he sat.

'What were you arguing about on the road?' he asked us very pointedly. There was silence. An awkward silence. We all knew what we'd argued about: Who was the best? Who was the greatest? Who was fittest to be leader? To be fair to us women, it was mostly the men, although Salome has some views about the issue. A few men glared at James and John who'd started the whole argument. Always ambitious. Always expecting to be better than the rest of us.

The teacher sighed and looked around at all of us, 'Haven't I told you again and again? Haven't I shown you so many times?' His expression wavered between exasperation and weariness. 'What do I have to do to get through to you? To show you? *It's not about being first.* If you're so keen to be first, then make yourself the last. If you want to lead, learn to serve', he said.

The children were playing around us. 'I've been trying to show you another world from that of the politicians and powerbrokers. The world I'm speaking of is not like that.' One of the toddlers approached the teacher. He reached out and sat him on his knee. 'Does this child worry about who is the best, the greatest? Do you think he has worked out a career trajectory for himself in my service? I'm talking to you about a godly kingdom, a rule of the sacred. You want to know about leadership in that kingdom?' he asked. 'It means being as simple as this toddler, as these children.'

Something to think about

'The core proclamation of Jesus focuses not primarily on human action but on God's actions, a final, definitive action totally beyond human control. Jesus' core proclamation is that the kingdom of God – that is, God exercising his power to establish his full, conclusive rule over Israel and over the whole world – is coming, indeed, is already present to some degree in Jesus' words and deeds, and will soon be present in all its fulness...

'... humans can do nothing to "hasten the coming of the kingdom of God", let alone "build" or "form" it. Jesus does not call upon his followers to create or form the kingdom of God. He calls upon them to respond to its inexorable coming and partial presence in his ministry. They do so by radically changing their lives according to Jesus' "halaka", his way of interpreting and enacting God's will in the Torah in the light of the culmination of Israel's history.'[103]

*

The reward of the kingdom is in living its way.

*

---

[103] Meier, Vol V, page 307.

'The identification between Sophia and Jesus leads to a new appreciation of the inclusive and universal liberating love revealed in the specific and limited person, Jesus of Nazareth... points to the incomprehensibility of God and specifically to the incomprehensibility of divine Wisdom.'[104]

*

'The God of the parables is compassionate beyond comprehension and cannot be controlled by any human notion of what is appropriate.'[105]

---

[104] Elizabeth Johnson, quoted in Edwards, pages 61-62.
[105] Denis Edwards, page 46.

8

Opposition Grows

Dome of the Rock, Jerusalem

Reading

Going to Jerusalem: Luke 9:51ff
His life was threatened: John 7:1, Luke 21:37-22:2, Matthew 26:1-5, Mark 14:1-2
Chief priests, elders and scribes look for a way to kill him: John 11:45-54

Place

In and near Jerusalem, the holy city, the centre of the Israelites' religion, and so, for Jesus, a religiously observant Jew, the physical centre of his faith.

Context

Jerusalem is a central focus for Jesus' faith and the temple is the most sacred place within the Holy City. As an observant Jewish teacher and prophet, Jesus made the journey to Jerusalem to observe the feasts as required in Mosaic Law, possibly three times during the three years of his ministry. Depending on his starting point, the distance could have been up to 130 kilometres. Taking weather and his route into account, the journey from Galilee to Jerusalem would possibly take three to five days.

This section starts by largely following Luke's account. Luke's Gospel along with the Acts of the Apostles is presented as a two-volume journey into faith and mission. Historical record was of interest to the evangelists in the early Christian community only in so far as the chronology of events illuminated an understanding and memory of the meaning of Jesus and what he meant to his early followers. Hence the significance of all four Gospels locating the events in this section in Jerusalem around the time of the Passover.

8.1 Facing Jerusalem

Place

The Gospels locate these events around Bethphage and Bethany (where his friends Lazarus, Martha and Mary lived), near the Mount of Olives, in the city and, finally, in the temple itself.

Context

8.1a reflects on Jesus' entry into Jerusalem as a drama in five acts as seen through the eyes of one of his close followers.

8.1a Decision

Reading

Jesus resolutely sets out for Jerusalem: Luke 9:51, Luke 9:21-22, 9:43b-45, 18:31-34, Matthew 20:17-19, Mark 10:32-34.

His fear is real. Dissent about his teaching has been mounting. He's been saying things to us about danger. There is good reason for him to avoid the city. He went there secretly once, not telling us, not even his family or Peter.

And then he returned – quiet and slow like an old man. Was he trying to gauge people's support for him? If it comes to the crunch, he must know that the sort of people who follow him will be too scared to defend him. He's not naïve.

At night he sits alone deep in himself. He is distressed. We know better than to disturb him. Does he think his time is running out? He says he will attend the Passover as usual.

> determined
> resolute, a rock
> willing himself forward
> he sets his face
> towards the city

This morning, something has changed. He has made up his mind. He is purposeful. We pack up our gear and start behind him on the road towards Jerusalem.

8.1b Preparation

Reading

The cost and means of discipleship: Luke 9:51 to 14:35

He talks to us as we walk. We are used to this now, his way of talking, pointing out simple things like trees that have no fruit or fields of wheat, always turning it round into something we hadn't seen before. Now, though, there is an urgency in the way he speaks to us.

I'm confused by this. So are the others. Why are we going to Jerusalem when he keeps saying there is danger there for us? All I can do is follow along, listen to him and maybe one day I will understand.

> I follow him
> step after step
> into fear
> I had not imagined
> the meaning of our journey

8.1c Consternation

Reading

Weeping over Jerusalem: Luke 19:41-44, Luke 13:34

It is spring. The air is clear and warm, weather that would normally make you sing. We see the city from afar. We pause on the Mount of Olives to take in the vista of the holy place. We've stopped here before; it is a favoured place to rest and savour the festival days ahead. We see the palaces, the fortress and the mess of rooftops where the streets and markets run. Above it all, the temple dome gleams, dazzling gold.

> his sadness
> washes out from him
> over us all
> across the stone-hard walls
> of the holy city
>
> he weeps
> for a city forgetting
> its people
> its eyes closed
> to a God of love

and for all who weep –
refugees camped in despair,
the lost and homeless,
all those who grieve
religion that betrays itself

8.1d Demonstration

Reading

Entering the city: Luke 19:28-40, Matthew 21:1-11, Mark 11:1-11, John 12:12-19, Zechariah 9:9

It is the Festival of Unleavened Bread, the Passover. There are groups like us moving along the roads towards Jerusalem. As we reach a village near the city, he sends a couple of us on ahead to borrow someone's colt. It seems he has this planned. What is he thinking?

Jerusalem is choked and noisy with people who have come for the festival. Into this, he rides, a man on a donkey, people cheering and racing after him. We are attracting too much attention. What is he doing? Is he mimicking the coming of Zion's king into the new temple after the return from Babylon? Or is he claiming something even more dangerous and serious?

The Roman soldiers are on every corner, showing their force, showing the fear the rulers have of riots and disturbances. He must know he is provoking the Jewish leaders, too, who are always trying to placate the Romans; he must know he is frightening them because the crowd who

hang off his words – the sinners, the ritually impure, the
beggars and rabble – might turn on them.

> *hosanna,*
> they cry *hosanna*
> to a dusty man
> riding a donkey's foal
> to a point of no return

8.1e Provocation

Reading

Cleansing the temple: Jeremiah 7:1-11, Luke 19:45-48, Matthew 21:12-13, Mark 11:15-17, John 2:14-16, Isaiah 56:3-8

Context

The story about Jesus cleansing the temple appears in all four Gospels. The event is charged with significance: it takes place in the temple as the Passover festival was bringing heightened crowds and tension into the city. There are resonances of the prophetic in the action and the words of Jesus. For those who know their scriptures, the evangelists' accounts cannot but evoke memories of the prophet Jeremiah.

Scholars have read this story at many levels. One cites at least three critiques Jesus might have been making: (i) of how Gentiles were being treated, which was inconsistent with Isaiah's vision of the temple as a place of prayer *for all nations* (Isaiah 56:7); (ii) of the financial abuses surrounding payment for sacrificial animals, which needed to be made in a specific currency and hence needed exchange; and (iii) of the increasing use of the temple precincts for political action by extreme Jewish nationalists.[106]

His follower's response

We follow him into the temple compound. This is a place of ambivalence for us. It is the holy place where the God of the Covenant dwells – the one place where we can offer sacrifice and be forgiven. It is also the place that represents the sell-out of the priestly class to the Roman oppressors: in return for keeping us docile, the priests keep their jobs with all their perks. They live in luxury at the expense of us who pay them tithes and tributes.

In the Court of the Gentiles, it is hectic. Travellers are changing their money for the temple currency; the crowd heaves and surges around the tables of doves and cattle and sheep. Temple security guards are everywhere. The Romans have their soldiers in the fortress overlooking the Court with its congestion, shouting and gibberish, the smell of animal dung and blood, and smoke from the sacrificial fires.

a scuffle
in a corner of the Court
brings screams
scrabbling for coins
tables turned –

---

[106] Taken from Peter Walker, *In the steps of Jesus*, Oxford, Lion, 2009, chapter 11.

the crack of whip
in the splinter of silence
his anger
bounces off the walls
of the watching fortress

and echoes back
the words of prophetic doom
from Jeremiah
in this treasured new temple
he has gone too far

children cry out,
sing joyfully
as children do
picking up their parents' mood
Hosanna, Son of David

8.2 Teaching and testing

Reading

Teaching in the temple: Luke 19:47-48, Luke 20ff
Criticising hypocrisy: Luke 20:45-47, Matthew 23:1-12, Mark 12:38-40, Matthew 23:13-24, Luke 7:36-50, 11:37-44, 11:45-54, 18:9-14
Evenings: Luke 21:37-38, Mark 11:11,19, Matthew 21:17, Psalm 17

Place

In the temple, Bethany, Mount of Olives.

In his ambitious work of restoring the temple, Herod had built up the surrounding land to increase the area of the overall temple precinct. At its heart was the Holy of Holies. Outside this sanctuary was the Court of the Priests, the Court of the Israelites (for ritually pure Jewish men), then the Court of the Women, and further out again surrounding the others, the Court of the Gentiles. The altar for burnt offerings was in front of the Holy of Holies.

Context

Teaching in the temple when the city is crowded with Passover pilgrims guarantees a large audience and maximum attention. It is also a powerful symbolic action: Jesus teaches in the holy city's holiest place during the most sacred festival.

Living as he did in a sectarian Jewish world that comprised a diverse range of religious beliefs and ideologies, Jesus necessarily took part in debates and discussions that various Jewish groups in his day had about the requirements of the Torah – what they meant and how they were to be applied to one's life. This is what rabbis did.

The Pharisees were such a group, a literate sect of devout lay Jews, who, in response to the hellenisation of Judaism around 150BC, sought to reform practice of the

Mosaic law. They were zealous in teaching the Torah and in promoting their legal reforms, especially around ritual purity (fasting, washing) and the Sabbath, and were keen to convert ordinary Jews to their way of observance.

They probably engaged in debate with Jesus, recognising what they shared with him: a fierce commitment to work towards all Israelites living according to God's will and so the Law and Prophets. In his confident and idiosyncratic approach to the Law, Jesus upsets some of them, such as his practice of eating and drinking with those considered sinners and impure (e.g. Luke 5:33-39) or his teaching against divorce which challenges 1CE practice. No-one takes kindly to being chastised, especially if they pride themselves on being religiously diligent in their observance of the Law. Some Pharisees were adversarial; some were aligned with Jesus, such as Nicodemus (John 3:1-12; 7:47-52, 19:38-40) or Simon the Leper (Luke 7:36-50). Saul (later Paul) was a Pharisee.

The Pharisees will not be involved in Jesus' trial and death.

8.2a Mint, dill and cumin

you polish
the cup outside
but not within –
*be generous to the poor,
and everything will be clean*

your flimsy tithe –
mint, dill, cumin, garden herbs –
in no way fits
your need to practise justice,
faithfulness and mercy

8.2b An uninvited guest

'that woman
weeps and strokes his feet,
hands all over him
you'd think he'd stop her,
send her on her way

'a man of God
would surely know her type –
but no, he simply says
*turn from your sin
and go in peace*'

8.2c Jousting with lawyers

with all the wiles
of their profession
they press him hard
with tricks of words
and threats of defamation

uninhibited
he returns the charge –
you levy huge costs
widows cannot pay, slam
shut their door to freedom

8.2d When you pray...

call no-one teacher
there is only one
and all are students –
one father only
who is in heaven

speak humbly
when you go to pray
unlike some teachers:
*do everything they say,
not what they do*

8.2e Ordinary folk

old women nod
and young men grin
to hear him say
the teachers do not practise
what they preach

he makes us laugh
and shuffle nervously –
telling teachers
that they strain mosquitoes
and swallow camels

with their tassels
and their flounces
they carefully
step around us
like muddy puddles

he dares
talk back to them
about a God
who cares
for folk like us

8.2f His close friends worry

he keeps telling
people they belong
in God's realm –
why won't he leave things be
and stop endangering us?

the temple spies
are watching him,
the Romans
don't take kindly
to this talk of empire

this is not the time
to take the elders on –
hang back
I want to say, *take care
don't mess with them*

is he just stubborn?
what drives his passion
and conviction?
after all this time
I still don't understand him

8.3 Last appeal to Israel

8.3a A great dinner

Reading

Luke 14:16-24, Matthew 22:2-10

Context

We assume Jesus told his stories in various ways to various audiences. Matthew's version of this story is more vengeful than Luke's, including the killing of the murderers and the punishment of those without wedding robes. Is Matthew's record one of the versions of the story in the way Jesus told it? Or has Matthew collapsed several stories together? Or is it an interpretation from the community at the time Matthew's Gospel was written 50-60 years after Jesus' death?

Not everyone responds positively to the invitation to join the feast. In Luke's account, the guests who have previously accepted the invitation all find excuses not to attend. Those who do attend are not the rich and powerful, but the marginalised, the poor, the hungry, the outsiders, the sinners.

In this way, the Great Dinner is a story of the reversal of expectations. However, in verse 24, Jesus goes further with the challenge to his listeners that an individual's response to him and his message will determine 'whether he or she will be admitted to the eschatological banquet, which is imminent'.[107] Jesus tolerates no excuses. It's a daring claim. No wonder he begins to court more open opposition.

---

[107] Meier, Volume V, page 373.

Response

What does this say of the host:
· that he opened his house and his wealth in a spirit of hospitality?
· that he wanted to eat and drink and celebrate with friends?
· that, when they readily accepted, he prepared with alacrity?

What might this say to the host:
· that one friend prioritised his newly acquired real estate above the host's company?
· that another friend valued being with his cattle more than enjoying the host's generosity?
· that a third chose to spend time with his new wife rather than bring her to meet his friend, the host?

And what might this further say of the host:
· that despite these rebuffs, he still chose to be convivial and generous?
· that, faced with these insults, he gathered other people around him?
· that, not deterred by his wealthy friends, he found delight in those who had little?

This is a host who takes delight in being in the company of people and sharing with them from his abundance in a spirit of joy and festivity.

8.3b A story about bad tenants

Reading

Mark 12:1-11, Matthew 21:33-43, Luke 20:9-18

Context

In the context of increasing pressure from the authorities (chief priests, elders and lawyers) who are questioning Jesus' authority and setting ways to trap him, Jesus' ministry is rapidly coming to an end. By likening himself (by association) with Jeremiah who predicted the destruction of the earlier temple, the heartland of Jewish faith, Jesus courted danger and accusations of presumption. This parable, possibly his last, told by Jesus within the temple precincts, has been described as a final warning to the temple insiders that 'they are in dire danger of playing out the role of their forbears, who in this holy city murdered the prophets God sent them'. Is he warning them about the consequences for them if they reject him? In the final violent end to the parable, the gospels report Jesus connecting with the prophets and with the son in the story. His story provokes the criticism: Who does he think he is?[108]

---

[108] Adapted from Meier, Volume V, page 374.

Response

> he tells a story
> of occupiers, squatters,
> in a vineyard
> robbing the owner,
> murdering his son
>
> the vineyard owner
> kills the evil tenants
> to avenge his son –
> *what do you think
> this story means*
>
> he asks the crowd
> looking pointedly at those
> who want to trap him,
> squirming at a tale
> directed to them
>
> his listeners
> clamour to hear more,
> his stories
> falling on their leaders
> like an avalanche

8.4 Finding strength and comfort

Under increasing pressure and knowing the forces were organising against him, each night he returns to Bethany or to the Mount of Olives.

> in a grove
> of thousand-year-old trees
> under ancient stars
> the intimacy of being
> held by the Eternal

> save me, Lord,
> hide me beneath your wings –
> lions surround me
> crouching under cover,
> hungry for their prey
>
> hear me, probe my heart
> and see I've walked your paths,
> show me again
> the wonders of your great love
> by your hand save me, Lord[109]
>
> bread and wine
> with friends – no need
> for explanation
> except to share
> fears of what might lie ahead

8.5 The Law and the Sabbath

Reading

Man with a withered hand: Mark 3:1-6, Matthew 12:9-16, Luke 6:6-11
Man with dropsy: Luke 14:1-6
Plucking of grain: Mark 2:23-28, Matthew 12:1-8, Luke 6:1-5

---

[109] Adapted from Psalm 17.

Context

What's the Sabbath for? What kind of God did Jesus promote? Jesus' approach to the law was one of common sense. The original Torah was less prescriptive than had developed at this time, especially through over-zealous groups among the Pharisees, some of whom in trying to compensate for the impact of foreign elements on the practice of Judaism, had become prescriptive and narrow in their interpretations. We can see something similar in some historic as well as some contemporary Christian pieties. Jesus teaches a more realistic observance and a more humane approach.

8.5a Almond blossoms

Reading

Healing of the bent woman: Luke 13:10-17

Place

A synagogue on the Sabbath.

Response

In July 2018, I was travelling on the local 231 Palestinian bus from Jerusalem city to where I was staying in the southeast of the city. At one of the stops, there was a very old woman. She had shrivelled with age and was bent almost double. She tossed her stick onto the bus and then clambered up using the rail and made her way to a vacant seat in the front. In the context, it was impossible not to recall Luke's story of Jesus healing a crippled woman, who, like the Palestinian woman on the bus, was bent and could not stand straight.

***

all I see
are stones and feet –
I can't remember
almond blossom against sky,
my grown-up grandson's face

I visit the synagogue because that is what I had always done on the Sabbath. Taking my place outside at the entrance because I am afflicted and unclean. We stand there in a group in our raggedness, a band of old and sick. The man Jesus is teaching there.

The women around me start to push me forward. The teacher has seen me and gestures towards me but, of course, I do not see him beckon. I stand before him, leaning on my stick, turning to go back. I don't like it, being there, before all the people, me an old woman. What do they think? I should not be here inside the synagogue, someone like me. I can't see his face, only his tunic and his feet in well-worn sandals.

'Woman', the man says, 'you are set free. You don't need to worry about this weakness, this twisting of your body'. Is he making fun of me? 'Stop it, Sir', I say, 'please don't mock me. I am old. Would you mock your mother if she were old? If some spirit afflicted her?'

'How long have you been like this?', he asks.

'Sir, so long. Since I was young, since my son became a man.' Then, I feel his hands upon my aching neck. And on the back of my head. Firm, he holds them there. And then, he grasps my shoulders, lifting them up slowly, slowly, till my back knits straight again; and then he gently raises my head, higher until I stand erect and look into his face. Still, I cannot see his face for all my tears and I am shaking my head back and forth, not believing what he has done. There in the synagogue, I laugh and cry, shout out to God for saving me.

The leader of the synagogue comes up to me and yells that I should not have come there on the Sabbath. If I wanted to be cured, I should have gone somewhere else another day. I simply came to worship. I didn't know I would be healed.

And they argue then about the Sabbath and should this man have healed me. The man called Jesus calls them names. He says I am more valuable than an ox or donkey and I should be freed, even if it is the Sabbath.

All the people seem to agree. They surge around. Noisy. Laughing at the synagogue leaders. Cheering for the healer, Jesus.

***

The watchers fell into two camps: his adversaries were confused, tongue-tied, out-of-argument; the 'people' (the mob, the ordinary folk) were 'overjoyed at the wonders he did'. Or was there not perhaps a bit of satisfaction that Jesus had bettered the legalistic detail-watchers? Of course, joy for the woman herself. Joy at the spectacle – something to run home and talk about, a bit of interest on the block. Joy at seeing officiousness put down.

> with a touch
> and words of kindness
> he undoes the bonds
> crippling imagination
> for new possibilities

Jesus' understanding of the Sabbath law left room for this kind of action.

8.5b The forgotten crippled man

Reading

John 5:1-18

Place

Jerusalem. The Pools of Bethesda, or in Hebrew, *Beth-Zatha*.

Excavations in the old city of Jerusalem near the stunning Church of St Anne show two large pools and several smaller pools near the north of the temple area in Jerusalem. There are remnants of arches there, evidence of the colonnaded porticoes. The pools are part of an intricate water system that once served the nearby Jewish temple and its rituals and were used as medicinal baths. Today, Lion's Gate (previously known as St Stephen's Gate) is near where the Sheep Gate originally gave entry to the city. *Bethesda* is said to mean *house of mercy*.

Context

John's Gospel recounts that while Jesus is in Jerusalem for a religious festival, he goes to a pool near the Sheep Gate. There he sees a man who has been waiting for decades, thirty-eight years – a man's whole life – to be made well. The author of John's Gospel locates this healing story of a cripple after the story of Jesus' interaction with the woman in Samaria and the healing of another of the son of a 'royal official' from Capernaum (John 4:43-54), two people from outside Judaism. It is followed by a long discourse on life, judgment and witness.

Regarding the significance of the pools and the man needing help, some ancient manuscripts later added the explanation to John 5:4 that the paralysed 'waited for the moving of the waters. From time to time an angel of the Lord would come down and stir up the waters. The first one into the pool after each such disturbance would be cured of whatever disease they had'.[110]

While this reflection focuses on the healing of the paralysed man, it is useful to note that John is also building the mood against Jesus in Jerusalem, as told in the second part of the story, the loaded exchange in the temple about the Sabbath.

---

[110] See note c, *New Jerusalem Bible*.

8.5c All kinds of paralysis

Thirty-eight years trapped and powerless: there are all kinds of paralysis. How many people have no one to help them to the pool when the waters are stirred?

I met a farmer recently who has inherited land from his father and his grandfather before him. He has the papers to prove it. Yet, there have been changes in government and in the lines between nations, so his land now stands in another nation from that of his grandfather.

For 29 years, he has been in the courts, submitting first one plan or map and then another; first one argument and then another; payment after payment, delay after delay, action and inaction. He cannot build on his land, but he tends it. He turns the dry soil and produces figs, grapes, wine and carob to make a living. The authorities have come and destroyed his trees, cutting down 1500 of them. So, he has planted 3000. To unlock this paralysis is a political act. The person who helps this farmer will stir the same kind of trouble Jesus stirred up in Jerusalem.

8.5d Stirring the waters

For some years, our parish was blessed with the ministry of a priest with cerebral palsy. Tim defied his condition with insightful homilies and an incisive wit. He won the affection and respect of parishioners, especially the younger members. One day, I needed a signature from him on some papers. Watching Tim manipulate the pen so that it connected with the paper gave me a small insight into the determination he needed simply to face the routine tasks of each day. If Tim had been beside the Pool at Bethesda, many people would have reached the waters before him.

Jesus' healing at the pool carries a revelation of 'God' for any one of us paralysed within our infirmity:

For all the Tims of this world with erratic unpredictable limbs
For those trapped in arthritis and its like
For amputees from war, road rage or raging infections
For the generation who limp with polio's legacy
For paraplegics and quadriplegics,
For those fighting their way back from stroke
For those with uneven legs, unreliable knees and rickety hips
For those with bent backs, stiff necks and pressed discs
For the limbless and the atrophied

For those paralysed by red-tape and bureaucracy
For those locked inside addiction and depression
For those locked outside fellowship by lack of language
For those who do not have access to those who might advocate for them, pull strings or simply accompany them to court or Centrelink
For those who have nearly given up hope

God is in Jesus
caring enough to notice
to pause, to ask,
to listen, hear –
then command him into health

Jesus in a white coat, in a nurse's cap, in a carer's touch, in a physio's firmness, in ceramic and silicone joints, canes, crutches, wheelchairs and mobility scooters, prosthetics, aids for turning on taps and doing up bras, chair lifts, handrails and ramps, thick, soft-soled shoes and paracetamol. Massage and medicine; counselling and company.

Jesus, by the authority within him, and moved by compassion, did this sort of thing.

When he did this sort of thing, Jesus claimed he did it in his father's name. Those who heard him understood that in doing that he was claiming his father was God. They were dangerous words.

Jesus' actions stirred waters that would turn into a flood against him.

8.6 A dutiful Jew with laws of love

Reading

Deuteronomy 6:4-9, Leviticus 19:16-18, Mark 12:28-34, Matthew 5:44, 22:34-40, Luke 6:27b, 10:25-37

Place

In Luke 10, the Gospel tells a story that refers to Samaria and its people. Samaria is a region north of Judea and south of Galilee on the western side of the Jordan. It is thought that, by the first century AD, a range of ethnic groups lived there, including non-Israelites as well as descendants of some of the Israelite tribes. Those who followed the religion of the Samaritans accepted only the Pentateuch and not the later writings of the Prophets. They also looked to worship on Mount Gerizim rather than Mount Zion as the Judeans did. There was animosity between the Samaritans and the Jewish people.

Context

In Mark 12, Jesus is teaching in the temple, in debate with some Sadducees, chief priests and scribes. Mark, writing for his community and their circumstances (some forty years after the death of Jesus), mentions that some chief priests and elders deliberately set out to trap him, sending some Pharisees and Hellenistic Jews along to join in the discussion. One scribe, appreciating Jesus' answers, asks him to name the greatest commandment.

In his reply, Jesus draws on his knowledge of the scriptures to go to the heart of its teaching, linking two texts to summarise the greatest commandment. The first is from Deuteronomy, the core creedal proclamation that opens the morning and evening Jewish prayer known as the *Shema*; the second is from Leviticus, detailing care for one's neighbour.

The scribe who has asked the question is impressed and there in the temple precincts respectfully acknowledges Jesus as 'Teacher'.

Elsewhere, the Gospels record how Jesus' wisdom about love went beyond word to deed, to embrace those beyond his immediate community, beyond friends to enemies.

8.6a Rabbi Jesus

Reading

Deuteronomy 6:4-9, 11:13-21, Numbers 15:37-41

The Shema is a touchstone for you and your listeners. I try to imagine you in your interactions with fellow teachers and with your followers. It is such a different world, a different time, a different culture with its layers of complexity. I can only see you through the lens of now: my time, my place, my own cultural potage.

> the tassels
> on your prayer shawl,[111]
> verses of the Law
> carried on your arm,
> written in your heart[112]

Mindfulness of God's Covenant and the Law...

> like photographs
> of my dearest loves
> I carry close
> always in my mind –
> as if I could forget

---

[111] See Matthew 9:20, 14:36, Mark: 6:56, Luke 8:44.
[112] See Deuteronomy 11:18, Numbers 15:37-41.

8.6b God's law of love

Reading

Deuteronomy 11:13-21

in the temple
as the *Shema* is invoked
he proclaims
Hear, O Israel
there is only one Lord

write this on your heart
and with your whole being:
love your God
and your neighbour
as yourself

the Torah teaches us
to speak no ill of one's own
nor harm our neighbour,
and without grudges
to love our brethren,[113]

speak of love at home
and with your children,
ponder love
while walking in the park
before you go to sleep,[114]

---
[113] Adapted from Deuteronomy 19:16-18.
[114] Adapted from Deuteronomy 6:6-8.

> he walks his path
> in step with Wisdom
> breathing in
> and breathing out
> a God of love

8.6c Who is my neighbour?

Reading

Luke 10:25-37

> Who observes this law of love?
> It is the stranger – and despised at that –
> who not in words, but action,
> lifts up wounded people
> takes care of their brokenness
> gives generously for their wellbeing
> holds them in their thoughts
> with kindness and compassion.
>
> Keep your eyes open, listen carefully
> on the streets, off the highways,
> quietly, without fanfare:
> there are many neighbours to be found
> in unexpected places...

8.7 By whose authority?

Reading

John 7:1 to 10:24

Context

The Sadducees, as distinct from the Pharisees, were a wealthy aristocratic priestly elite around the first century BC and the first century AD. They were theologically and politically conservative, tending to align themselves with the Roman rulers of Palestine. This compromise of loyalties, their wealth and the power it gave them made them unpopular with ordinary Jewish people. They were often in conflict with the (lay) Pharisees, and they took a hardline in their rulings on the Law, which for them finished with the Pentateuch. Their power was centred around their predominance in the temple and the priests. A 'no-body' (cf John 9:29) as free and charismatic as Jesus would have given them cause for alarm.

Ultimately, the people with power to intervene against Jesus in his mission were those associated with the temple and the ruling power: the Sadducees, the High Priest Caiaphas, the Roman Prefect Pontius Pilate and various priestly, scribal and aristocratic officials around Caiaphas.

And, of course, one of the Twelve who would betray him, Judas.

8.7a Challenges

Reading

John 7:53 to 8:11

Place

Jerusalem, temple area.

Context

The preceding sections gives some context for this memory in John's Gospel. Jesus had stayed deliberately in Galilee, sending his family on to Judea for the festival of Sukkot. Later on, he goes up to Jerusalem quietly.

During Sukkot, or the feast of Tents (Tabernacles), pilgrims build temporary shelters (*sukkot*) from palms and willows as a reminder of being people of the Exodus, on the move, in temporary shelter for 40 years guided by God through the desert to the land of Israel. It is a festival over seven days, requiring pilgrimage to the temple. As an observant Jew, Jesus went and observed his obligation.

During the Sukkot festival, there was a water ceremony each morning invoking God's blessing for rain in good seasons. The water was taken from the Pool of Siloam and carried to the temple. There were ceremonies of light with dancing and music, feasting and study of the Torah (Law).

John's chapter 8 begins with the authorities threatening to stone a sinful woman and ends with them threatening to stone Jesus.

8.7b A woman

Jesus has spent the night on the Mount of Olives. It is just dawn when, once again, he comes to the temple. Before long, people gather around, to hear what he has to say.

It is not long before the legal experts arrive with their latest test for him.

>   they drag her
>   through the crowded court
>   shamefully
>   they parade her weakness
>   expose their malice
>
>   in their hands
>   they roll and rub
>   warmth into flint-edged
>   stones – not as hard
>   as the words they hurl at her
>
>   and he
>   for a moment, holding still
>   her trembling terror,
>   ignores them, bends down
>   and scribbles in the dirt
>
>   'the Law says this
>   the Law says that –
>   what's your view on this?'
>   *stone her, then, but only
>   if you've not sinned yourself*

> one by one they leave
> till he stands with her alone –
> I don't judge you,
> turn around and find
> all you seek within

And what of the lawyers? Perhaps they learnt a little about compassion that day also.

8.7c Challenging Jesus

Reading

Isaiah 55:1-3, John 7:37-39
Luke 20:1-8, 20-26 ff, Matthew 21:23-27, Mark 11:27-33

Context

The reference from John's Gospel is situated during the Festival of Tabernacles. John uses this feast to situate Jesus' teaching about living water. His words reference readings used in the festival (cf Exodus 17:1-7, Ezekiel 47:1-12, Zechariah 14:8-9). John recognises in Jesus eternal Wisdom.

Division and criticism are building. He claims that his teaching is not his own and challenges them: 'Anyone who resolves to do the will of God will know whether my teaching is from God' (John 7:14-20). Quite a statement. His confidence that he speaks on behalf of God and not just on his own assertion – or delusion – is disturbing and frightening.

Response

On the last day of the festival, Jesus is teaching as usual in the temple. He continues teaching with determination.

> he stands up
> and cries out: *listen*
> *if you are thirsty*
> *come here, hear me,*
> *my words are living water*
>
> is he crazy
> or possessed?
> men take sides,
> women argue
> for him and against
>
> is he the one
> the one who is to come
> the one we're waiting for?
> how can he be the one:
> he comes from Galilee
>
> they ask him
> dangerous questions –
> 'in whose name?'
> 'by what authority?' –
> questions of the powerful
>
> authority
> comes from within
> he taught
> unsettling the certainties,
> established hierarchies
>
> he's so persistent
> in his message,
> almost taunting them
> despite the danger –
> why can't he just be quiet?

8.7d A blind man testifies

Reading

John 9:1-41, Isaiah 42:1-7

Place

Near the Pool of Siloam and around the temple.

Context

In verse 9, the Gospel notes that 'Siloam' means 'one who has been sent', a descriptor that the author of John's Gospel favours in speaking of Jesus. In this account, John's Gospel brings together Tabernacle festival symbols of water and light (sight) and relates them to Jesus as himself being the source of these blessings.

Response

His disciples saw the man as blind because of sin. Jesus saw the man.

> go and wash
> in the Pool of Siloam
> he tells a blind man
> laying hands
> upon his eyes
>
> night is coming
> when, like this man,
> no-one will see
> unless they fix their vision
> on God's light in me
>
> *if this man*
> *is not from God*
> *he could do nothing*
> the man who once was blind
> sees things in their true light

The Jewish leaders punish those who think Jesus is messiah. They turn on the once-blind man and throw him from the synagogue.

8.7e Is he blasphemous or merely mad?

Reading

John 10:22-39, Psalm 27, Psalm 30

Place

In the Portico of Solomon, a colonnade running along the eastern side of the temple precinct.

Context

This time, John situates his story in winter, that is, November or December, around the feast of Dedication (now known as Hanukkah or feast of Lights) and about two months after the feast of Tabernacles. It is an eight-day festival commemorating the re-consecration of the re-built temple following the persecution by the Syrian ruler Antiochus in 168 BC. During the feast, houses and synagogues are illuminated and Psalm 30 is recited. Healers and prophetic teachers were not uncommon in first century CE.

Response

>   *my teaching*
>   *is from God*, he says –
>   scandal
>   ricochets
>   off temple walls
>
>   the leaders
>   hem him in
>   with their demands,
>   ridiculing
>   baiting him

we hear
of other healers
changing lives –
this man heals,
claims God's name

we hear
of other prophets
here and there –
this man claims
he is God's son

we hear him
stirring up the crowds
with claims
he and God are one
... that is blasphemy

I cry for mercy
Lord be my help
save me from the pit
do not let my adversaries
gloat in triumph over me[115]

And they pick up stones in righteousness against him.

8.8 Betrayal

Reading

Mark 14:10-11, Matthew 26:14-16, Luke 22:3-6

---
[115] Adapted from Psalm 30.

Place

Jerusalem.

Context

All that has gone before. All that is about to happen.

Response

> When was it that you crossed over in your mind
> from friend to someone who saw him
> only as a curiosity? Was it when he persisted
>
> in his provocations? Or when you saw the elders
> lifting stones against him? Did rumours he was crazy
> worry at your own divided self?
>
> You could have simply left Jerusalem and gone back
> to doing what you did before, or were you already
> too much changed by him? Were you angry
>
> that he'd infiltrated you and fired up your hopes?
> Did you feel he'd sucked you in? Revealed
> desires you'd prefer kept hidden?
>
> So, you choose to go into the gloom,
> looking for a chance to turn him in...
> In this dark space, your mind is tuned to focus

on his weaknesses and vulnerabilities
while the rest of us keep watching out for him,
getting food, making sure he rests, and shoring up

among ourselves our own faltering confidence,
all of us surging up and down between amazement
– yes, he still surprises, even now – and deep dark fear.

Your eyes flicker between your contacts in the temple
and the rest of us, pretending life is normal.
Don't you know that, in their eyes,

you are already fouled: you are one of his,
his followers? Don't you see? They'll take
whatever you can give,
then you'll be tossed aside?

Something to think about

'Jesus treated the Law with sovereign freedom: tightening it in some respects (especially divorce) but relaxing it in others. The fact that he may have agreed with the Sadducees against the Pharisees on certain issues illustrates that interpreting the Law was an essential occupation for many Jewish intellectuals, so as to root it in the realities and possibilities of people's lives. Nobody would have worried about the principle of interpreting the Law; some may have worried a great deal about the details of how it was interpreted.'[116]

*

---

[116] Martin Forward, *Jesus: a short biography*, Oneworld Publications, 1998, page 107-108.

John Meier speaks of discovering a Jesus as someone who 'presented himself to his fellow Palestinian Jews as the eschatological prophet in the mould of Elijah, sent to Israel at the climax of its history to begin the regathering of the whole people, a people prepared for the coming of God's definitive kingdom by a radical doing of his will according to the Torah as interpreted by Jesus.'[117]

*

'Jesus' prophetic act was surely intentional. His entry into Jerusalem on the back of a donkey said more than many words could. Jesus is seeking a reign of peace and justice for all, not an empire built through violence and oppression. Mounted on a small donkey, he appears to the pilgrims as a prophet, the bearer of a new and different order, in contrast to the one imposed by the Roman generals on their war horses. His humble entry into Jerusalem becomes a satire and mockery of the triumphal processions organised by the Romans to take possession of conquered cities... As a public act proclaiming a nonviolent anti-kingdom, it would have been enough to lead to a decree of execution.'[118]

---

[117] Meier, Volume V, page 372.
[118] Pagola, pages 340-341.

9
Last days

Mural, village of al-Eizariya, identified as the village of Bethany

9.1 Raising Lazarus

Reading

John 11:1-54

Place

Bethany was the home village of Jesus' friends, Lazarus, Martha and Mary. Bethany is about three kilometres from Jerusalem, (but not so straightforward to reach these days). There is a site there that is honoured as the burial place of Lazarus. Like other burial places of Jesus' time, this is a cave cut deep into rock. The entrance is low and leads by narrow winding steps to what is remembered as the burial area itself. To enter that cave is to enter into a chilly darkness; to climb up the steps and come from the tomb is to be blinded by light in the warmth of the sun.

Context

This account of the raising of Lazarus appears only in John's Gospel and is the seventh – and the climax – of the *signs* that Gospel ascribes to Jesus. The previous *signs* included the wedding in Cana (2:1-12), cure of an official's son (4:43-54), cure of a paralysed man at Bethesda (5:1-15), feeding 5000 (6:1-15), walking on water (6:16-24) and cure of a man born blind (9:1-41). In John, this last *sign* catapults Jesus into the passion. The length and detail of the story signals its significance. The details in John's account make it powerful and touching.

It is interesting to reflect on an Aramaic version of the Lord's prayer, which translates 'forgive us' as 'unbind us as we unbind each other'. In this story, Jesus unbinds Lazarus in the most extreme way.

9.1a Time to respond

Reading

John 11:1-16

Friendship

> every minute
> is suspended here –
> this threshold
> between your whole life
> and its end

If you had a friend, a very close friend, someone you trusted and felt at home with, and you heard they were ill, what would you do? Surely, you'd contact his family. Or if your friend's sisters, who were also your friends, with whom you'd shared meals and companionship, sent you a message saying he was ill, surely, you'd try and reach them. You'd check the date and time of the message: how long since it was sent? What might have happened to your friend since then? And surely, you'd read the subtext of their call: please come, we need you here.

Yet, when two women friends send Jesus word that his good friend Lazarus is ill, he hesitates. Two days. The news might well be three days old by now. He knows it will take another three or four days to reach their home. Anything might have happened in that time. Yet he waits two more days.

were there things
you had to finish off
in Galilee –
knowing that when you left
this time would be your last?

or were you
steadying yourself
against the threats
knowing to go to Bethany
meant going so much further

finally, you admit
your friend has died:
*let's go to him
and in his death
let God be glorified*

9.1b Martha

Reading

John 11:17-37, Luke 10:38-42

You are more than acquaintances. You are almost-family, tied by mutual affection. You have found refuge and comfort in their home, this household of Martha, her sister Mary, and their brother. You've been close enough to enter the inevitable disputes of family life. Remember that time Martha invited you for a meal...

flustered
and dusted with flour
she complains –
her sister sits attentive
to every word you say

*Martha, Martha,
don't fret about the food:
what matters
is I'm here now, come,
sit down, and talk with me*

if you wish
to nourish others
with bread and care
let the yeast rise –
God's word in you

    Now, you finally reach their village, and you hear what you already know: Lazarus died some days ago. Someone rushes in to tell the sisters. Martha knows how long it has taken you to come. She and Mary have been watching the road, waiting for you to come. Now the house is filled with mourners, friends and neighbours bringing tears and food and comfort. You should have been here two days ago.

Martha rushes out
greets you, flushed and trembling,
*where have you been?
if you'd been here, she cries,
my brother would not have died*

You speak to her of resurrection. She assents to this.
And then, going further, you tell her in her grief, *I am the
resurrection. I am life. Believe in me and you will never die.*

> her brother's body
> cold, bound and buried
> deep within a cave
> Martha cries out her faith
> in the Messiah, Son of God
>
> (multi-tasking
> in the kitchen
> she must
> have been listening
> to him after all)

'I believe you are the Messiah, the Son of God, and you are here in this our village.'

9.1c Mary

Reading

John 11:28-30

The understanding between sisters. A wordless glance from Martha, and Mary knows Jesus has come. She slips away as quickly as she can, her sadness lifted by her anticipation of seeing him. Glances flit around the room – watching her with care. Is she going back to be alone by Lazarus' tomb? How distraught his death has left her. With womanly concern they follow her.

          he delayed
     and now he's come
      and calls for her
       he's waiting for her
    there outside the village

         she falls down
       at his feet, weeping
        sadness, anger, joy
       in tears of consolation
       the intimacy of grief

          she does not see
         her women friends
          who lift her up –
          she sees his tears
    and knows he shares her pain

       Take me to him, Jesus says.

9.1d Companionship

For those who have accompanied me in my grieving,
For those who have been there to let me weep
For those who have lifted me from the cavern of loss
For those who have understood my isolation and bereft-ness
For those who have simply listened and wept with me
For those who have given me the solace of friendship
I give thanks.

For the times I have been able to share the intimacy of others' grief
For the times I have been asked to share their fears of death
For the times I have wept with others, not just for my own dying
I give thanks.

9.1e Unbinding

Reading

John 11: 38-53

> in the darkness
> of my tiny room
> who sees me?
> who believes enough
> to call me into light?
>
> tied up in knots
> within my own confines
> who cares
> enough to unpick
> cords that bind me?

As you approach the tomb, you are deeply moved: sadness, yes, and pain, at the death of a loved friend, and how that is affecting his family. What else? Is there, too, some fear, knowing that your next actions will seal your fate with the religious leaders in Jerusalem? Some anger that this is how it is finishing?

Practical as ever, Martha bustles beside you. 'It is four days already, his spirit has already left, and he will stink.' Martha, Martha! You know what you must do.

> some men
> toss aside their cloaks
> to roll away
> the stone that blocks
> sunlight from the deep cold cave

You face the fears and darkness of the cave. And giving glory to your Father God, you call out loudly into the gaping maw, *Lazarus, come out.*

> in his tomb's dark womb
> Lazarus hears the call to life
> the only way
> is step by narrow step
> of passage to the threshold
>
> *unbind him,*
> *let him go free,* you command
> amidst the stench
> God calls us out and sets us free
> even if we don't know we're dead
>
> O Thou,
> from whom the breath of life comes...
> give us wisdom for our daily need,
> detach the fetters of faults that bind us,
> as we let go the guilt of others[119]

9.2 Plans for his death

Reading

John 11:45-54, 12:9-11

It is as you expected. Word runs into Jerusalem, into the temple. The chief priests and the elders call a special meeting. Your actions, now, are not just blasphemous: they

---

[119] This verse is adapted from the Aramaic 'Our Father'.

disturb the tenuous balance of power and politics in Judea. The Chief Priest himself is appointed by the Roman rulers. *If we do nothing to stop this man, everyone will believe in him. And the Romans will even take over the temple.*

> he emerges
> unbound and untombed –
> how can
> a man's freeing
> be seen so dangerous?
>
> the establishment
> ignores the miracle of life
> seeing only
> the threat he poses
> to their hold on power

9.3 Dinner at home with friends[120]

Reading

John 12:1-8

The anointing of Jesus by Mary, sister of Lazarus, appears only in John's Gospel. The synoptics include a story of Jesus being anointed by a woman, but that is in the home of Simon, a Pharisee, and the woman in those accounts is a woman with an unsavoury reputation. The location of this in the home of Jesus' friends makes this a very different story.

---

[120] Some of the events described in chapter 8 may have taken place in this week leading up to Passover.

Six nights before Passover, Martha's household throws a dinner in honour of Jesus. It is an evening of warmth and closeness. Lazarus is there, of course, in some ways joint guest-of-honour with Jesus himself. The Twelve are there and maybe some of the family's closest friends, but it is a private and sombre celebration, planned to draw no public attention. It is now well-known that the authorities are looking out for him and have ordered anyone who finds him to report it. Jesus is a wanted man.

Martha prepares the food – surely putting on some of her special dishes as a way of expressing her joy for the return of Lazarus. Mary, too, has her own way of expressing what she feels. The precious ointment that she uses to anoint Jesus is worth, in Judas' estimation, almost the equivalent of a year's wages for a labourer.[121]

>   a few days ago
> he walked into their sadness
>   confusing her
>   with consolation,
>   her brother's restoration
>
>   she's listened well,
>   treasuring his words –
>   tonight
>   she senses in him
>   fear for what's ahead
>
>   she casts aside
>   her customary veil
>   and modesty –
>   her hair tumbles loose
>   as she kneels near him

---

[121] To offer a comparison, in 2021, the minimum annual wage for workers covered by an award in Australia was around $40,000.

brimming with her love,
spills the precious nard
from an alabaster jar
intimately
she anoints him

fragrance
permeates the house –
the extravagance
of her recklessness reaches
every corner in the town

the money-counters
call her profligacy
a scandal –
Jesus reads her heart,
accepts what she has done

Something to think about

'In his every action Jesus' aim was to give glory to his Father (John 7:18); that is, to reveal God's faithful love... every word he spoke and every work he did manifested in some way his glory. This is especially true of those special actions of Jesus that John calls 'signs'...

'(The seventh sign) comes as a climax to the other six and gathers up their main themes in a powerful act when Lazarus comes out of the darkness of death (John 11:43), is freed (11:44) and given life (11:25-26). It is also the climax of Jesus' public ministry. It is, in John's account, the action that finally caused the religious leaders to decide to kill Jesus (John 11:45-54).[122]

*

---

[122] Fallon, pages 249-251.

'Jesus' followers unbind Lazarus and in so doing they ignore the old law, for they touch what is ritually unclean. By acting on Jesus' command, they accept the new law of the new covenant. They act as the agents of Lazarus's liberation from death and the imprisonment and darkness of the tomb. We, too, as followers of the risen Christ, must be agents of liberation.'[123]

---

[123] Brian Purfield, 'The raising of Lazarus,' in Thinking Faith, 27 March 2020, https://www.thinkingfaith.org/articles/raising-lazarus

10

Passion and death

Ancient olive trees in the Garden of Gethsemane, Jerusalem

10.1 Final meal with friends

Reading

Luke 22:15, John 13:1

Place

There is a room in the Old City of Jerusalem that is regarded as the possible site of this final meal of Jesus with his friends. It is, indeed, an 'upper room', above what is regarded by some as the tomb of King David. It may well be the 'guest room' mentioned in Luke and where the disciples stayed after the death of Jesus, or at least, gathered. Like many other sacred sites, it may, or may not, be the original building that a connection of Jesus made available for him and his friends to gather for their final meal together. In some ways, that doesn't matter. What is remembered from that night is what is important for us.

Context

The meal Christians remembers as the 'last supper' took place around the year 30 CE on the day before Passover during the 14-day festival of Nisan, the first month of the Jewish calendar which falls around March-April. While the synoptic Gospels suggest the Last Supper was a Passover meal, John is clear the meal took place the day before Passover. And while Jesus might originally have intended to celebrate Passover with his friends, the meal became instead a final meal together as Jesus sensed the authorities' hostility mounting against him.

There were theological reasons for linking this meal with Passover: in their telling, the evangelists associate this meal with the banquet to celebrate the coming of the Messiah foretold by the prophets (Isaiah 25) the new Covenant God has forged with his people through the blood of the new Passover Lamb (Exodus 24:3-11, Jeremiah 31:31-34, Hebrews 8, Hebrews 9:18-21) and the Wisdom of God embodied in Jesus (Proverbs 9:1-5).

The earliest version of this event is the one recorded in 1 Corinthians 11:23-26 although Paul was not one of those who had travelled with Jesus and did not know him in the flesh.

10.1a Longing to spend time together

How many times do meals feature in Jesus' story? Meals can be times of closeness, times of the very ordinary; they can be vehicles for celebration, settings for significant events and announcements; sometimes, meals can become times of dissent and division. During his public ministry, Jesus did not discriminate with whom he ate, sometimes eating with those who were considered 'unclean', and so scandalising some observers. This last meal that Jesus had with his friends would have elements of all of these.

I once worked with a woman who was a remarkable educator and leader. Too early in life, she developed cancer. She fought it valiantly – furiously – for three long years, until her death. During the last months of her life, for reasons that are not relevant here, access to her was restricted and information about the seriousness of her condition was controlled. Consequently, when she died, many of those who had known and admired her were caught off-guard, because they had not had the opportunity to express to her what she meant to them. I have always felt that was a loss both to the woman and to her friends and colleagues.

Jesus did not rob himself, nor his chosen disciples of this opportunity. He deliberately organises a meal during which he will demonstrate his affection for them in action and word and allow them the opportunity to enjoy this last meal of fellowship and closeness with him.

The reflections below are fictionalised imaginings of that evening through the eyes of a woman disciple.

10.1b Preparation and Premonition

Reading

Mark 14:12-16, Luke 22:7-15, Matthew 26:17-19

A disciple reflects

He's arranged accommodation with someone he knows, someone with some means, where we all can stay while we're in Jerusalem. He sends us women on ahead to get things ready for the Passover.

We find the room tucked well away above the street up a flight of stairs. It is spacious and set up ready for us when we find it. After the bustle of the market and the streets, it's quiet, a kind of refuge here. After all that's been going on, I'm feeling relieved.

> around the hearth
> we shape the dough
> kneading memories
> into the bread we'll share
> later with each other

While we are working, Peter rushes in. 'There's been a change of plan. Don't worry about tomorrow's meal. Just do something simple for tonight'. Mariam of Magdala asks, 'Why? What's happened?' Peter glances towards the Teacher's mother, Miryam, and shrugs: 'That's what he said'.

***

Early in the evening, the men return, Jesus, the Twelve, his brother James. The room fills with their noise and bluster. Some of them are arguing. Jesus lets them be for a while. Then, as they take their places for the meal, they quieten.

do you know, he asks,
watching each of us in turn,
how much I've longed
to be here to share
Passover with you?

my friends,
my dearest friends,
my chosen ones,
I'll observe my Passover
when the kingdom is fulfilled

tonight
I know some of you
will let me down
one will hand me over
to those who want to kill me

angry silence
swathes the room
muffles questions,
gentling the men
to kindness with each other

10.1c Teaching by example

Reading

John 13:1-17, 1 John 2:7-8

Context

I learnt when living in India to remove my sandals before entering a house, so as not to bring dirt from the roadway inside. The same practice is maintained in many countries, such as Philippines, Thailand, Laos and households of people from these backgrounds now living in Sydney and Ballarat and all around the world.

In a similar fashion, it was a common practice in first century Palestine for a person to wash their feet as they entered a house. If the household was a wealthy one, then feet would be washed by a servant.

Through a woman's eyes

We had already served the wine and olives to the men when Jesus stands, removes his cloak and pours water into a basin.

> black-winged kites
> catch on a draught mid-sky –
> fingers poised
> above the salted parsley
> arrested by his action

he goes to John
to James and Philip
one by one
washing their feet
just like a slave

Peter, of course,
bumbles and protests –
then bows humbly
in confusion
to accept the gift

and then he kneels
before us huddled women –
he takes in turn
our swollen calloused feet
and washes them

do you know, he asks,
*what I your teacher
have just done?
as I have done
so must you*

10.1d Blessing, breaking bread and sharing

Reading

Matthew 26:26-30, Mark 14:22-25, Luke 22:14-20,
1 Corinthians 11:23-26

Response

>blessed are you Lord God
>in the gifts of your creation –
>drink this cup
>eat this broken bread,
>do this remembering me

>he tells us
>to remember him
>as though he's leaving,
>going somewhere else,
>just when we've come so far

>we've had many meals
>together – quiet, simple, noisy,
>some well-catered ones –
>I can't sip even water
>without recalling him

>blessed are you Lord
>in the gifts of your creation –
>drink this cup
>eat this broken bread,
>do this remembering me

10.1e Discourse

Reading

John 13:31 to 16:33, Exodus 12, Galatians 5:22

Response

    Something big is happening here –
    hard to put my finger on it –
    a quiver in my chest, my breathing slow
    and slower. Do the others feel it too?

    See the men reclining at the table –
    all attention on him:
    the chitter-chatter, banter, tom foolery,
    has stopped – the usual guffawing, backslapping,
    grumbling – gone.

    We women too are quiet – sitting still, here by the
    cooking pots –
    not fluttering around the table as we usually do –
    We are on the edge of something and he
    speaks as though all the things he hasn't said
    till now must now be said.

***

he speaks to us
of love, of comfort, peace,
of being with us
in his Spirit
trying to assure us

a woman screams
throughout the hours
of giving birth –
she holds her child,
forgets the pain

and so, he warns,
if he must leave us
even so
he won't abandon us
like children left on streets

farewell, my friends,
he says, farewell –
a knife
cuts through my chest
tears me apart

I will be with you
in my Spirit
and you will know
my Way
by listening to Her

don't be troubled
I'll be with you
I wish you peace
trust me
as you trust God

love each other
as I have loved you
let this mark you out
and you will be joyful –
I want you to be happy

you will suffer
they'll reject you
from their churches
take heart, they hated me
because I spoke the truth

don't worry –
we are as close
as the branches
of a vine
are to the vine itself

my parting gift
is peace
a peace that only I
and my Father
can give you

10.1f He prays for us

Reading

John 17

Response

> now I know
> how the leper felt
> when he was healed
> how the blind man felt
> when he could see:
>
> in this room
> amidst remnants of the meal
> that we prepared
> he prays for us
> and blesses us
>
> my skin prickles–
> I want to hold forever
> every word
> yet in a day or two,
> I'll forget some
>
> he speaks of love
> and of his Father –
> he means God –
> and love for us...
> no-one has touched me like this
>
> all my life till now
> I've done my duty
> faithful in most things –
> when he speaks this way
> I feel myself dissolve

he rises –
it's time to go, he says,
the men leave with him
for the Mount of Olives
where, Judas knows, he likes to pray

It has become quite dark.

10.2 Abandonment

Reading

Jesus foretells Judas' betrayal: John 13:21-30, Matthew 26:14-16, 20-25, Mark 14:18-21, Luke 22:21-23
Jesus in the Garden: Mark 14:32-42, Matthew 26:36-46, Luke 22:40-46, Hebrews 4:15, Psalm 6:1-3, Psalm 43
The betrayal: John 18:1-11, Mark 14:43-52, Matthew 26:47-56, Luke 22:47-48

Place

From the lower city of Jerusalem, you can see across the Valley of Kidron to the Mount of Olives. The modern-day Mount slopes from the dark shadows of cypress pines down the unshaded cemetery of Jerusalem. At its base is Gethsemane, a grove of olive trees which give their name to the garden. Some of the twisted trunks of olive trees are said to be up to 2000 years old, having renewed themselves from their base with new shoots over the centuries.

Worn stone steps have been uncovered leading from the city near the Church of St Peter in Gallicantu down to the Kidron Valley. Some scholars agree that Jesus and his close disciples walked these same steps to go from the Upper Room on Mount Zion to cross the Kidron and reach the garden at the foot of the Mount of Olives where he liked to spend time.

On the two occasions I have trod these steps, I have been moved deeply by the sense that these steps were actual steps that Jesus might have taken after his farewell meal with his friends, again after his arrest and yet once more after a night of imprisonment and physical punishment. Why does this move me so much when knowing the actual site of other moments in Jesus' life seems less important? Perhaps, it is that they are a detail, a small element in the largeness of the Passion. Like a good poem, the steps call out to me.

Context

By way of summary in a well-known story, the events of Jesus' passion and death appear to have followed this timeline:

- farewell meal with his friends
- arrest the same night
- examined by Jewish officials in the house of Caiaphas, the High Priest in 30 CE. (Mark and Matthew mention both a night trial and a Sanhedrin meeting the next

morning; Luke mentions only a morning meeting; John refers to a hearing by Annas and then by Caiaphas.)
- handed over to the Roman governor, Pilate, early on Thursday or Friday. (Only Luke includes Pilate sending Jesus to Herod, the Jewish procurator of Galilee who happened to be in Jerusalem at the time. When Jesus refuses to answer his questions, Herod sends him back to Pilate.)
- crucified and buried the same day, the 'day of preparation' for the special Passover sabbath, that is, Thursday or Friday. He was about 36 years old.

The words used in the Gospel of Mark to express Jesus' state in chapter 14, verses 33-34, have been variously translated as 'terror and anguish' (NJB), 'distressed and troubled' (NIV), 'distress and anguish' (NCB) and 'distressed and agitated' (NRSV). The words used have associations with something traumatic and unanticipated, with 'profound and sudden shock', a physical as well as an emotional reaction; distress that is overwhelming. Jesus goes on to plead that he is so overwhelmed he could die from the grief and sadness he is feeling. These few lines call up our amazement and silence.

Watcher in the garden

Who are these men who are entering the garden in the darkness? What is their business here at this late hour? Wait. There is a leader. He stops and speaks to those with him, then leaves them sitting near the entrance while he moves deeper in among the olive trees with just three of his companions.

Once more he pauses. Turns, speaking to the men beside him, as his words drop into the darkness. He asks them to wait with him and keep guard.

> the weight
> of all the centuries
> of these olive trees
> presses down on me
> with agonising sorrow

His three friends stand there, watching him. Look uncertainly at each other. Then they settle on the ground and pull their cloaks around them as once more he moves away into the shadow of the trees.

> I'd like a friend
> to come and sit with me
> no need for words
> in times of terror
> your company is what counts

After a short while, the man returns to his three companions. They have fallen asleep. *Simon, Simon*, he cries, *wake up, keep watch with me*.

> shadows shift
> across the garden
> with the breeze
> small gusts stir
> fear among the olive trees

Who is this man, who seems so desperate? He once more leaves his friends. A few metres away, he opens wide his arms as if in prayer, then falls prostrate to the ground. His body shudders; distress wracks him; he seems totally abandoned.

> *have mercy, Lord,*
> *my body is in anguish*
> *I've lost my strength*
> *how long before*
> *my agony is done?*[124]

Through his pain, he calls out to his father. Talking to him, pleading with him. Poor fellow, calling to an absent dad. Surely, he knows there's no-one else around. His friends are here, of course, but they are fast asleep, again. I have never seen anything or anyone so solitary.

He goes once more and wakes them up. His voice sounds less angry than sad as he asks, *Can't you stay awake with me, just this once?* And leaves them once again for his solitude.

> It is worse at night:
> the fears, the pain, the grief
> darkness sharpens
> the sense you are alone
> and there's no way out

A third time he returns and finds them sleeping.

But now, something is happening. There is movement near the entrance. Lights and the sound of heavy feet along the path. He wakes them up. *It's time to go,* he says.

A crowd approaches – ruffians, it seems, with swords and clubs. Police? Security? Someone steps forward from the crowd, goes up close towards the man and embraces him

> memories
> of what we've shared
> your kiss tonight
> smears on my face
> the odour of betrayal

---

[124] Adapted from Psalm 6.

The guards and police take the man away. I know where they are going now: back across the Kidron up the Mount to the house of Caiaphas.

> in the olive grove
> shouts and flaring torches
> rupture the darkness –
> odd, the fear roused by a man
> who seems so ordinary

He stands gravely still and dignified. Where are the friends who came here with him? Surely, they are somewhere, standing by this poor forsaken man. No, I cannot see them. They have fled into the night.

> *vindicate me*
> *against a faithless nation,*
> *rescue me,*
> *O God, my soul,*
> *keep strong your hope in God*[125]

10.3 Trial

Place

The church of St Peter in Gallicantu ('Cock Crow') is a powerful place to visit. The artworks elaborate on Peter's denial of Jesus and his distress immediately afterwards at having failed him when he was in greatest need. One large mural features Jesus gazing directly at Peter. Jesus' hands

---

[125] Adapted from Psalm 43.

are bound in front of him, Peter's hands are fluttering, at a loss. Behind them the context of the meeting is spelled out: men and women sitting around a fire, a prison tower, high walls and in the middle, a tall pillar on which sits a rooster. Underneath the inscription from Luke 22:57 is irrefutable: non novi illum, 'I do not know him'.

Context

It is considered that the Church of St Peter is the likely site of the house of Caiaphas, the High Priest mentioned in the Gospels. It was at the house of Caiaphas that the Sanhedrin convened. This was the supreme judicial and ecclesiastical council of the Jews in Jerusalem under Roman rule. And so, it is likely that it was here that Jesus was brought after his arrest in the garden.

All four Gospels include the story of Peter denying his association with Jesus.

10.3a 'I do not know him'

Reading

Peter's denial: Luke 22:54-62, Mark 14:66-72, Matthew 26:69-75, John 13:38, 18:15-18, 25-27

Denial

I merge into the crowd following the temple police and elders back up to the High Priest's house. Someone I know, one of our group, manages to get me through the gates and into the courtyard.

>I squat
>beside the fire
>trying to stop
>my shivering
>and confusion
>
>from the brazier
>in the darkened courtyard
>hands pass fire
>giving each shadow
>a fearful name

I sit there silent with the guards and servants.

>I never thought
>it would be this way:
>you've passed
>into the system now
>a common criminal
>
>you led me on
>and I threw in my lot –
>talk along the shore
>said I'd lost my focus
>in taking up with you
>
>you moved me
>I believed you,
>loved the promise
>in your words of being free,
>purpose given to my days

Someone by the fire sitting opposite, says, 'Hey, aren't you one of them that goes around with the Nazarene? The fellow they've finally brought in?'

        I look away
    from the fire of attention
       feigning glare
  would I be next in chains?
'Who? No, I don't know him.'

    a girl, a servant,
    points at me, stares,
  peering through the flames
     'come on', she says,
  'don't lie, you're one of them'

   'you're wrong,' I say
  moving off towards the gate
    but she won't let up
  'you even talk like him –
you both are country bumpkins'

  'get this in your heads,
stop your stupid blathering –
for God's sake, strike me down
  give a man some peace:
    I do not know him'

Hours go by and morning is approaching. In the distance, I hear a cock crow, twice. Just then, the police lead Jesus out through the courtyard. As they near the gate, Jesus turns and looks straight at me.

     firelit faces
  huddled against the cold
    sick to my gut
I want to smash those words
I said: I didn't know you

Much later, in the bitterness of shame, I remember what Jesus said to me in the presence of the others at our last meal together...

> Simon,
> I have prayed for you:
> may your faith thrive
> turn your sorrow back
> to courage for your brothers

10.3b Here is your king

Reading

John 18:19-24, 19:42, Mark 14:53-65, 15:1-47, Matthew 26:46-27:61, Luke 22:47 to 23:56, Psalm 22

Places

The High Priest Caiaphas' house where the Jewish Sanhedrin sat: my visit to the underground cells thought by most scholars to be the site where Jesus was kept overnight beneath the High Priest's house leaves me disturbed and chilled.

Praetorium: the seat of the Roman governor, Pontius Pilate. Golgotha: a rocky outcrop shaped like a skull outside the city walls, so it would not defile the holy city. Passers-by would walk past the criminals hanging on their crosses. Jesus was crucified on the charge of being a political agitator.

Crucifixion was not used for Roman citizens. It is believed that this actual site lies beneath the Church of the Sepulchre, which, with changes over time, is now within the Old City of Jerusalem.

During the evening and next day, Jesus moved from the Upper Room to the garden, was taken back across the Kidron up into the city to the High Priest's house, across to the Praetorium of Pilate and then to Golgotha. The whole area of Jerusalem at this time was approximately 1000 metres by 1500 metres, so the distances between these places were not unduly long, but neither were they flat or straightforward. Certainly not for a man who had been tortured, deprived of sleep, and carrying a heavy wooden beam.

Context

The core details of the passion are that Jesus underwent trials by the Jewish and Roman authorities, was tortured and crucified. Some details within that larger story vary, for example that he met with the former High Priest Annas (John) as well as the High Priest Caiaphas or Herod (Luke) as well as Pilate. The synoptics (but not John) include details about Jesus being helped by Simon of Cyrene, comforted by women (Luke), Jesus being mocked while on the cross, the admissions by the centurion, and the darkness and tearing of the temple curtain following Jesus' death. John's Gospel focuses on Jesus as king, especially through the interrogation by Pilate and on the crucifixion itself. Unique to John's account are his words to his mother and the piercing of Jesus' side.

Consistent with his purpose of showing Jesus as the fulfilment of the Law and prophets, Matthew's account employs allusions to Hebrew scriptures that would trigger associations and new interpretations with his largely Jewish audience. On the other hand, writing around 70CE, Mark emphasises for his probable audience of Gentile converts, that Jesus is a prophet, the Messiah in the most unlikely of circumstances. For Luke, the journey to the cross is the climax of Jesus' journey to Jerusalem from where the new religion will spread, whereas John's much later account, completed around 100CE, continues through his lens of the *Word* and the *Wisdom of God* present in the gradual assertion of Jesus' unique relationship with the Father. For John, the crucifixion is the final realisation of the hour in which God's glory is revealed.

Response: What do the passion and death mean?

The four Gospels offer four different perspectives on this question. They are only four of a multitude. Before the theology, the ecclesiology and the hermeneutics, there is the suffering human person, Jesus, a Jew of the first century CE with a divine mission – for me a story too big for any one person to grasp.

- At some point, he realised his actions and teaching would get him into strife: that mainstream religious groups would oppose him, that the powerful and those in government would give in to pressure to get rid of him: after all, he was critical of the religious establishment.
- He threatened their power because he spoke in a way which resonated with the powerless, the mob, the unruly, the less desirable which in turn threatened to

- destabilise the working balance between religious leaders and Roman governors.
- He was a thorn in the government's side, speaking of a new kingdom, a new empire.
- As a fellow Rabbi, he was an irritant and an embarrassment to some Pharisees.
- One step after another led to the inevitable climax: his 'hour'.
- He wanted to leave a memorial for his friends – that which had marked him and his disciples out from John the Baptiser, had outraged scribes and pharisees... eating and drinking with those most in need of God's mercy and friendship. 'Just keep doing what we've been doing these past years'.[126]
- In his suffering he felt abandoned by his friends and even by God.
- He did not resile from his teaching and conviction about God and what that meant for religious people.
- The gradual crystallising of his sense of his mission, formed in his intimacy with the divine – apparently now a failure. In the garden – and long before – a demon he must have had to face.
- He maintained his grace and dignity.
- He was treated as a political agitator, killed outside the city, rejected, an undesirable.

---

[126] Greg Wilson, correspondence.

10.3c Before Pilate

Reading

John 18:28 to 19:16a

After a night of being questioned, held in captivity and an early morning trial before the Jewish elders, Jesus is taken to the palace of Pilate in the centre of the city.

> I visit the place
> of his captivity –
> the cold terror
> of that dark pit
> chills my blood

The Jewish leaders do not enter the Palace because it is Passover. They wait for the Governor to appear.

> espousing
> the letter of the law
> they keep their hands pure
> happy for the foreigner
> to do the dirty work

Pilate comes out to meet the elders. They transact their business outside the palace.

> a simple act
> of state business:
> name the charges,
> make your judgment,
> use your own law

Having attempted to dismiss the Jewish leaders in classic bureaucratic style, Pilate goes back into the building. He cannot dismiss the image of Jesus quite so easily. He summons the prisoner inside and speaks with him.

> this talk of *kingdom* –
> are you threatening the Empire?
> do you really think
> you are the type to rule,
> be king of all the Jews?

> *my kingdom*
> *is from another place* –
> *I don't want my friends*
> *to take up weapons for me*
> *but testify to truth*

> *you say*
> *I am a king:*
> *all who love the truth*
> *recognise the truth*
> *in what I say*

'Who knows what truth is?' retorts Pilate.

Again, the governor goes outside to the waiting religious leaders, giving them his verdict: the charges should be dropped.

> he hits upon
> an exit strategy
> through the mess
> he can try and save himself –
> not this blameless man, nor truth

To appease the mounting tension outside the palace, the governor walks with Jesus back inside and somewhere, in the damp dark regions of the palace, has him flogged.

> too demeaning
> for a Roman to endure,
> too cruel
> for Jewish law to allow,
> they flog his guiltlessness
>
> they know he's doomed –
> so, after thrashing him
> thugs take leave
> to ridicule and mock him
> slap him across his face

Once more, Pilate goes out to the gathered Jewish leaders. The crowds would be building, all those visitors for Passover, the curious, the concerned, the appalled.

> in a purple rag
> and plaited crown of thorns
> he stands there
> found innocent
> and condemned

Pilate is increasingly troubled. The crowds are restive. The Jewish leaders are adamant. If word of this gets back to Rome, his head will be on the block. Yet, there is something about Jesus that confounds him. Again, he instructs the soldiers to lead the prisoner back inside the palace. 'Who are you? Where are you really from?' he asks. 'Answer me.'

> outside
> the religious leaders
> speak of Caesar –
> within the room Jesus
> speaks of power from above

Finally, Pilate returns outside. Time is passing and a judgment – if one is to be made – needs to be made soon.

> the chief priests claim
> their only king is Caesar
> in the judge's seat
> Pilate listens to the crowds
> and not his better self

Pilate hands him over to be crucified.

10.4 Death and burial

Reading

John 19:16b-37, Matthew 27:33-56, Mark 15:22-41, Luke 23:33-49

10.4a Crucified outside the gate...

Was it from anger with the Elders for forcing his decision? Or a weak attempt to restore himself? In one last gesture of defiance Pilate insists on what he has written:

> in languages
> that everyone can read
> a sign –
> Jesus of Nazareth
> King of the Jews

10.4b Faithful to the end

Faithful to the end, the women accompany him, even here to this barren rock stinking with failure and death.

>   Miryam
> who carried
> and cherished him,
>   now bears
> wrenching sorrow
>
>   Mariam
>   from Magdala,
> a tower of strength
> dependable as always
> by his mother's side
>
> Mary, Clopas' wife,
> Salome and other
> followers throughout
> Galilee and now
> attending him in death
>
> he asks kindness
> from his dearest friend
> for his mother
> will mother all
> who follow him

10.4c The End

At the end, the awful end, Jesus screams out demanding to know why even God seems to have forsaken him. Mark introduces the opening words of Psalm 22, and we are expected to imagine all the verses that follow. In a shorthand way, Mark is saying, 'Yes, there was unimaginable desolation, but just as the psalm moves from lament to a song of trust in God's goodness, so Jesus in his dying moments, moved to a point of consolation'. *He has done it. It is finished.* In Luke, Jesus invokes Psalm 31 in his moment of death. This psalm is recited as a night prayer by devout Jews. The evangelists want readers to remember Jesus speaking the name of God in the moment of his death.

> into your hands
> I entrust my life
> my faithful God
> you hear my cry for mercy
> when I call to you for help[127]

> *Elōi, Elōi,*
> my God, my God –
> from my mother's womb
> I've trusted in you...
> it is done – my God[128]

10.4d Waters of life

Reading

John 19:31-37, Zechariah 12:10

Response

Water. It calls out to all our thirsts in the heat of summer, our longing in the middle of drought, our desperation in a wildfire inferno. It is our lifeline, our lifeblood. It cleans. Renews.

And so John, after his witness to the terrible moments of Jesus' death, adds something more to his testimony in

---

[127] Adapted from Psalm 31.
[128] Adapted from Psalm 22.

verses 31-37 of chapter 19, in a way that would remind his readers of God's action in the past.

at Horeb
while his people wavered
Moses struck the rock –
water to quench their thirst
and quell their discontent[129]

a soldier's spear
pierces him to the core –
his mother,
overwhelmed with sadness
is flooded with his blessing

blood and water
gush from his heart,
diluting
the salt of our tears,
in an outpouring of joy[130]

come to me
if you are hungry
if you are poor –
whatever you thirst for,
come and drink your fill[131]

from here
the sea's immensity
reaches round the world –
in the vessel of his days
the Wisdom of Infinity[132]

---

[129] Exodus 17:1-6.
[130] Isaiah 12:2-4, John 4:14.
[131] Isaiah 55:1, John 7:37-39.
[132] Sirach/Ecclesiasticus 15:3, 24: 25-29, Psalm 36:9-10.

10.4e Once more the garden...

Reading

John 19:38-42, Mark 15:46-47, Matthew 27:57-61, Luke 23:50-56

Joseph of Arimathea and Nicodemus, a Pharisee, are men of some means. Both have followed Jesus secretly. They are emboldened to ask Pilate for Jesus' body, so they can provide him a dignified burial.

>not just a death –
>it was a calculated
>killing
>of compassion
>and all small hopes
>
>after the crowds leave
>darkness covers us
>in silence
>grey as a corpse
>your absence is everywhere
>
>two friends
>anoint your brokenness
>with cloth and myrrh –
>they place your body
>in a fresh-hewn tomb
>
>Mariam and I
>stay to watch the grave
>being sealed
>heavy stone dragged
>across our breath

iridescent
sun sets
at the end
of my road home
a house of shadows

awake all night
I push back
against the dawning
that nothing is the same,
nothing can be the same

yet, still
sparrows flit around the walls,
poppies still shine
rubescent on stone
... as they always have

Something to think about

'We preach Christ crucified, a stumbling block to Jews and a folly to Gentiles.'[133]

*

'The first of all believers, the Mother of Jesus and the Beloved Disciple, are given to one another as Mother and Son. "And from that hour" they become one. The centre of the cross scene is the foundation of the church, the formation of a new family, which cuts through all bonds of flesh and blood, but which is based on faith and love. It is, however, important to notice that the term "mother" is mentioned five times in (John) 19:25-27. The evangelist wishes to make clear that the "Mother" of Jesus becomes the "Mother of the Church" at the cross of her son.'[134]

---

[133] 1 Corinthians 1:22-23.
[134] Francis J. Moloney SDB, *The Living Voice of the Gospel*, Collins Dove, Melbourne, 1986, page 196.

11

Resurrection

Sculpture of St Peter, Capernaum

11.1 Mariam, first witness

Reading

John 20:1-18

Place

We return to the garden where the tomb is.

Context

Once again, we read the Gospel of John's lovely attention to detail: it is masterly, enticing and very human. At other times in his elaboration of his theology, he is quite abstract. All evangelists have Mariam of Magdala going to the tomb first. In most accounts, she is in the company of various other women. Mariam of Magdala – the tower holding the others together – becomes the first apostle of the Resurrection.

In the last section of Mark's Gospel – thought to be a later addition – Mariam returns to the other mourning disciples who dismiss her experience of Jesus (Mark 16:10-11). This reluctance to believe in the power of life over death later earns them a rebuke from Jesus when they experience him for themselves as they gather around the table for a meal (Mark 16:14). In Luke, the eleven and all the rest of the disciples judge the report from Mariam and the other women as 'an idle tale' (or 'pure nonsense' in the *Jerusalem Bible* translation) which they simply don't believe. However, in Luke, Peter has second thoughts and runs to the tomb to see – and be amazed – for himself (Luke 24:9-12).

Response

>
> impatient, restive
> she ties up in a cloth
> the balm and spices –
> sleep belongs to those
> who've reason to wake up
>
> she makes her way
> through empty darkness –
> defenceless
> against the firestorm
> of searing memories:
>
> how he'd surprised her
> with his words and actions,
> his fierce resolve,
> gentleness in healing,
> the name he used for her
>
> carrying sadness
> from her cold hearth
> like ash
> she waits by his grave
> blinded by the rising sun –
>
> he calls her name
> among the twisted olives
> shadowing the tomb
> sealed within grief she hears
> only a stranger's kindness
>
> the question
> stirs memories
> of the lake –
> *who are you looking for?*
> his invitation to disciples

> *Mariam,*
> he calls, and she sees,
> 'Rabbouni' –
> nothing further
> needs be said

11.2 Walking away

Reading

Luke 24:13-35

Place

While I am in Jerusalem, the wonderful librarian where I am staying encourages me to visit Abu Gosh. My checking of local buses makes the journey seem very complicated and drawn-out, making it difficult to achieve in the time available on my last Sunday in Israel. So, I miss the visit. On reflection, in the spirit of Luke's story, I should simply have walked.

Abu Gosh is one of four sites just out of Jerusalem that is considered a possible location of the Emmaus mentioned in Luke's story. This is based on the distance of '60 stadia' (about 11.3 kilometres) and supported by archaeological explorations and name derivations. Of the four disputed contenders, Abu Gosh, Al-Qubeiba, Qaloniyeh and Emmaus-Nikopolis, some scholars favour Qaloniyeh (near modern Motza) as the original Emmaus. Nikopolis is 160 stadia (or around 29 kilometres from Jerusalem making it difficult for the disciples to walk there and back in the one day. Qaloniyeh might be more favoured, but my librarian friend is very convincing and Abu Gosh is obviously an important place for her. Whichever is correct, 11 kilometres each way is a walk easily completed in less than a day.

Context

After Jesus' death, many disciples had already returned home to Galilee. In his story, Luke specifically mentions Cleopas as one of the disciples walking to Emmaus. The other disciple remains unnamed. Some scholars suggest the other disciple might have been Cleopas' wife, Mary, who, in John's Gospel, had remained by the cross. This view gives us an image of a couple returning to their home together after their time travelling with Jesus: imagine how they might have reflected together on the previous months culminating in the last few days. As with much else in the Gospels, we don't know who the other disciple was, and as with much else, it doesn't matter. Luke's story has its own purpose, and the precise identities of the disciples in it are immaterial.

In his powerful piece on Holy Saturday, James Hanvey reflects on the strange desolation of the place we know as waiting; how we instinctively want to avoid the stillness, the vacuum that refuses to be dissolved, the reality of the finality of death, the terror of our own impotence.[135]

On the road. A reflection in three voices

How strong that bond between us as we grieved these last few days – closer than brothers, closer than family. Just this morning, we were one of them. We called ourselves disciples.

> *Why her? So good. Too young. We need her.*
> *Now she's gone. And we are left alone.*
> *Sad, hollowed out, untethered.*

we leave them,
walk away from those
who use his name –
I wear my sadness
like a heavy cloak

We thought he'd come with might and power. The one we've waited for. No. They've killed him. Publicly humiliated. The women say they've seen him, and his tomb is empty. What would they know?

> *My dream dissolves. Damn fool. I put myself out-there.*
> *Thought I'd make a difference, following a hope*
> *for something better. The powerbrokers*
> *ridicule my attempts as*
> *trivial do-goodery.*

---

[135] James Hanvey sj, 'Holy Saturday' in *Thinking Faith*, 29 March 2013, https://www.thinkingfaith.org/articles/20130329_1.htm Accessed April 2019.

> commuters rush
> heads bowed
> against the wind
> someone slows his step
> and keeps his pace to mine

A stranger joins us as we walk. He lets us talk. How come he has not heard the horrors of these days? He gets us to explain what we had hoped for, asks us why, then asks us to recall the words of prophets from our scriptures. It's talk that gets me thinking why I ever dreamed of might and force and armies.

I weep for love turned dry. I'd hoped I'd found the one. The one who understands me. That we would give each other joy in travelling through the known and the strange as one. Instead, the bread we break in separate rooms is soured with salt.

> present as my skin,
> unnoticed as my pulse
> quickening
> with the rhythm
> of a lover's breath

In his company, as we talk, I hear my voice in his. Sense emerges from the words. I can almost see the upturned reasons for a crownless king: a hurting servant, without chariot or horses, but a gentle touch and quiet voice.

He takes my backpack from me – loaded down with failure and self-blame. As we talk, he takes the stones out one by one and lays them down, building stepping-stones to lead me forward.

> alone tonight
> my way stretches
> through desolation
> longing to be touched
> by a stranger's compassion

At our door, although we've just met, we sense we are about to lose a friend. We ask him in. He stays. A simple meal – some bread, a glass of wine.

> *Something has happened. Someone met my sorrow,*
> *my confusion, my sense of shame and failure.*
> *Someone spends some time with me.*
> *Does more than say, 'Huh, huh'.*
> *Someone seems to want to hear my pain.*
> *Surprised. I hadn't thought this person*
> *would do this – to join my sadness:*
> *take it on and weep with me.*
> *It isn't that we share some wine –*
> *but with this person, wine makes sense.*

> alone tonight
> my way stretches
> through desolation
> longing to be touched
> by a stranger's compassion

We are alone. My companion cannot stop smiling. The women are right, then. We wrap the balance of the bread, we grab our staffs and start straight back again the way we just have come, towards Jerusalem.

> *We share food, and in a stranger's features*
> *I glimpse a friend. I am re-claimed.*
> *There are things that I must do.*
> *I turn around, renewed.*

meeting his absence
in our emptiness
we discover him
*hallowing all
our times of waiting*[136]

a stranger
astounds us
on the way
can I bear the likelihood
you might see him in me

11.3 Back home in Galilee

Reading

John 21:1-25

Place

On the shore by the sea of Galilee. For Matthew, it was on a mountain, a cue for his readers that this was a revelatory moment, akin to Moses, the site of the Beatitudes, the Transfiguration, the mount of Golgotha. Luke's Gospel does not return to Galilee but concludes with Jesus leaving the disciples near Bethany not far from Jerusalem.

---

[136] This phrase and some ideas inspired by James Hanvey sj, 'Holy Saturday', inter alia.

Context

The Gospels recount various times and places where the disciples, in various combinations, experience the presence of the risen Jesus. On some occasions, it is while the disciples are having a meal: in the fellowship, domesticity and sheer ordinariness of eating together. This is one of the key memories they carry forward into their new life as the group of those who believe and follow his way: Jesus, the son of God, is present with them in the simple breaking of bread.

The evangelists emphasised two other post-resurrection convictions: (1) Jesus entrusted his followers with the mission to keep doing what he had begun, to go out and spread what he had taught them about the God of their faith and of the prophets; (2) in continuing his work, Jesus wanted his followers to do so, confident and assured that he would be with them, always. This message needed to be repeated because his disciples were alarmed and afraid (Mark 16:5, 8). (It is on this note that the original Gospel of Mark finished.) 'Do not be afraid' is a recurring phrase in the memories of the resurrection. (Matthew 28:5,10; Mark 16:6; Luke 24:36-38; John 14 at the Last Supper; Acts 18:9-10)

In John's account of the breakfast by the sea, there is a lot of agenda crammed in: a message of abundance of fish; another meal shared, more bread broken; and a second chance for Simon Peter.

Simon Peter

He told us to return. To go back to Galilee. And really, where else was there to go?

back home
now strangely familiar
changed
the way I see things
after all that's happened

back to a place
that reminds me
of the day
I wholeheartedly
agreed to go with him

back when
his words and actions
were the sun
rising with a promise
of a kind new world

back before
he brought down the wrath
of those in power
and I pretended
I didn't know him

back here
grief carves itself
inside me
there is space
only for regret

There are seven of us down by the Sea. Where else to go, but back to the water, back to the boats. This had been my life before it all began. With nothing else to do, we decide to go fishing.

not surprisingly
we caught no fish
all night
we talked and wondered
what he wanted of us now

A man wandering along the shore calls to us, as people do, asking about our catch.

> we haul
> our empty nets
> onto the boats –
> a meagre catch
> of fish... and men
>
> in morning sun
> on that gravelly shore
> when he cooked fish
> and gave us bread to share,
> we knew it was the Lord

After we eat, he turns to me. I am uncomfortable. The glance he gave me on the night that I betrayed him is scratched across my mind. It wakes me up at night.

> he looks at me –
> I turn my eyes away
> to search out clouds
> as though I had to check
> the weather on the lake
>
> *Simon*, he says,
> *do you really love me?*
> 'Yes' is easy
> but very hard to say
> knowing I've let him down
>
> three times
> I denied I knew him –
> three times
> he let me say I loved him:
> I knew I was forgiven

11.4 Peter

Reading

Acts 4:1-12 (and many other places in Acts)

Place

Back in the temple, in Solomon's Colonnade. Where Jesus had taught and provoked the authorities; the holy centre of the Hebrews; the institutional heart of the Jewish nation.

Context

This is some of what happened next as outlined by Luke in the Acts of the Apostles, the story of the disciples following the death, resurrection and ascension of Jesus. The story of the early disciples in the emerging church tells us something more about the Jesus they were following.

Fresh with memories of him, they came together: they taught (at Pentecost, speaking to the longing in each person's soul for the reign of a merciful, life-giving God); they healed; they lived in community; they worked out their 'way' – sometimes through disagreement and listening in communion – and they remembered him in the breaking of bread. Such a humanising God. Such a grounded divinity, meeting us in each other, in listening and engagement and in fellowship and food.

And the way they began then becomes a Camino that is always unfolding, always having to find its way, always a pilgrimage.

Response

It is Peter's joy that captivates us in
this story of healing and preaching.
It is Peter's total clarity and conviction
in Jesus and his teaching.
It is Peter's wholehearted commitment
and strength of discipleship.

> before the rulers
> before the powerful
> Peter rejoiced
> in proclaiming
> Jesus the Nazarene

Something to think about

'The story of the passion and resurrection of Jesus was the earliest piece of coherent story-telling that the early church used in its preaching.'[137]

*

'Only in the silence of Holy Saturday can we see the true terror of the cross. It exposes the ultimate source of the secular gods' power – the god of this world, the god of

---

[137] Moloney, *Reading the New Testament in the Church. A Primer for Pastors, Religious Educators and Believers.* Mulgrave: Garratt Publishing, 2015 page 147.

despair; the god who can crucify God. On this day, all our dreams fall away, our hopes scatter like dust in the wind; the fragile world we build of meaning, of goodness, of love, is only a poor, ragged shelter in which to hide from the frozen dark of an endless night. If we have the courage to place our ear to the silence of Holy Saturday we will hear a savage laughter. It is the gods of this world laughing at our hope for a saviour.

'There is also the guilt: could we have done something? In the space of Holy Saturday we have to live with all our betrayals... On Holy Saturday we live the limits of our love. We do not stop loving, but even though our love may be endless, we know it cannot be enough. We love now in pain, in longing; we love now on the cross of our own finiteness...

'In the emptiness of waiting, we begin to learn something that the god of this world cannot bear, the knowledge that it does not want us to know: at the very point of our failure and betrayals, when we taste our own impotence and limit, if we are not afraid to live in his absence, we discover him.'[138]

---

[138] James Hanvey SJ 'Holy Saturday: Waiting to cross over', in *Thinking Faith*, 29 March 2013.

Selective Reading Guide

Andersen, Frank, msc, *Jesus: our story*, HarperCollinsReligious, Melbourne, 2001

Brown, Raymond E., Joseph A. Fitzmyer and Roland E. Murphy, *The New Jerome Biblical Commentary*, Prentice Hall, Englewood Cliffs, NJ, 1990

Brueggemann, Walter, *Finally comes the poet*, Fortress Press, Minneapolis, 1989

del Nevo, del Mathew, 'Desert Literature, Desert Language,' in Michael Griffith, Ross Keating (eds). *Religion, Literature and the Arts Project: Conference Proceedings of the Australian International Conference 1994*. Sydney: Australian Catholic University, 1994 https://openjournals.library.sydney.edu.au/index.php/SSR/issue/view/849/ pp. 102-108

Edwards, Denis, *Jesus the Wisdom of God*, St Pauls, Homebush, 1995

Fallon, Michael, msc, *The four Gospels. An introductory commentary*, Catholic Adult Education Centre, Sydney, 1981.

Hanvey, James, sj, 'Holy Saturday: Waiting to cross over,' in *Thinking Faith*, 29th March 2013, https://www.thinkingfaith.org/articles/20130329_1.htm

Jewish Museum of Australia, *The Jewish Context of the Life and Words of Jesus, Teacher Notes*, https://www.jewishmuseum.com.au/wpcontent/uploads/2018/07/JLOJ_teachernotes___280618.pdf

Johnson, Elizabeth, csj and Susan Rakoczy, ihm, *Who do you say that I am?* Cluster Publications, Pietermaritzburg, 1997.

Levine, Amy-Jill, *Short Stories by Jesus*, New York, Harper One, 2015.

Martin, James, sj, *Jesus, a pilgrimage*, HarperOne, New York, 2014.

McBride, Denis, cssr, *Jesus and the Gospels*, Chawton Hampshire, Redemptorist Publications, 2002.

_____, *The Parables of Jesus*, Redemptorist Publications, Chawton, 1999.

Meier, John, *A Marginal Jew, Rethinking the Historical Jesus. The Roots of the Problem and the Person*, Vol I, Yale University Press, 1991.

_____, *A Marginal Jew, Rethinking the Historical Jesus. Mentor, Message and Miracles*, Vol II, Yale University Press, 1994.

_____, *A Marginal Jew, Rethinking the Historical Jesus, Companions and Competitors*, Vol III, Yale University Press, 2001.

_____, *A Marginal Jew, Rethinking the Historical Jesus, Law and Love*, Vol IV, Yale University Press, 2009.

_____, *A Marginal Jew, Rethinking the Historical Jesus, Probing the Authenticity of the Parables*, Vol V, Yale University Press, 2016.

Moloney, Francis, sdb, *Reading the New Testament in the Church. A Primer for Pastors, Religious Educators and Believers*. Mulgrave: Garratt Publishing, 2015.

_____, sdb, *The Living Voice of the Gospel*, Collins Dove, Melbourne, 1986.

_____, sdb, *Woman: first among the faithful*, Dove Communications, Melbourne, 1984.

Murphy-O'Connor, Jerome, *The Holy Land*, Oxford University Press, 3rd Edition, 1992.

Pagola, Jose A, *Jesus. An historical approximation*, Convivium Press, Miami, 2009 (2015 edition).

Pixner, Bargil, *Paths of the Messiah*, Ignatius Press, San Francisco, 2010.

Purfield, Brian, 'The raising of Lazarus,' in *Thinking Faith*, 27 March 2020, https://www.thinkingfaith.org/articles/raising-lazarus

Schlusser-Fiorenza, Elizabeth, *In memory of her*, SCM Press, Tenth Anniversary Edition, London, 1994.

Thurston, Anne, *A time of waiting. Images and insights*, The Columba Press, Dublin, 2004.

_____, *Knowing her place, Gender and the Gospels*, Paulist Press, New York, 1998.

Ungunmerr, Miriam-Rose, Dadirri, 'Inner Deep Listening and Quiet Still Awareness,' https://www.miriamrosefoundation.org.au/dadirri/

Vatican Commission for Religious Relations with the Jews, 'Notes on the Correct Way to Present the Jews and Judaism in Preaching and Catechesis in the Roman Catholic Church', June 24, 1985 https://www.bc.edu/content/dam/files/research_sites/cjl/texts/cjrelations/resources/documents/catholic/Vatican_Notes.htm

Walker, Peter, *In the steps of Jesus*, Oxford, Lion, 2009.

www.ingramcontent.com/pod-product-compliance
Lightning Source LLC
Chambersburg PA
CBHW011316080526
44588CB00020B/2725